J. K. Rowling – A Biography

A former national newspaper columnist who now works as a freelance writer, Sean Smith began his career with local newspapers in the West Country, before moving to London, where he spent ten years with the *Daily Mirror*, and a further two-and-a-half years with the *Sunday People*. He left to launch his own medical magazine, and it was this taste of editorial independence that led him to become a full-time author.

His first book, *Sophie's Kiss*, appeared in 1997 and became an international bestseller. It was followed by *When You Walk Through the Storm*, about the Hillsborough football tragedy, *Stone Me!*, a Rolling Stones companion, and the highly-acclaimed *The Union Game*. His most recent work, *Royal Racing*, was published in 2001.

Described by the *Independent* as 'a fearless chronicler', he is a veteran of countless TV and radio programmes. Like J. K. Rowling, he comes from the West Country, although he now lives in London.

Also by Sean Smith

Sophie's Kiss
When You Walk Through the Storm
Stone Me!
Royal Racing

J. K. ROWLING
A Biography

Sean Smith

ARROW

Published by Arrow Books in 2002

1 3 5 7 9 10 8 6 4 2

Copyright © Sean Smith 2001, 2002

Sean Smith has asserted his right under the Copyright, Designs and Patents Act,
1988 to be identified as the author of this work

First published in the United Kingdom in 2001
by Michael O'Mara Books Limited
Revised edition first published in the United Kingdom
in 2002 by Arrow Books

Arrow Books
The Random House Group Limited
20 Vauxhall Bridge Road, London, SW1V 25A

Random House Australia (Pty) Limited
20 Alfred Street, Milsons Point, Sydney,
New South Wales 2061, Australia

Random House New Zealand Limited
18 Poland Road, Glenfield
Auckland 10, New Zealand

Random House (Pty) Limited
Endulini, 5a Jubilee Road
Parktown 2193, South Africa

The Random House Group Limited Reg. No.954009

www.randomhouse.co.uk

A CIP catalogue record for this book is available from the British Library

Papers used by Random House are natural, recyclable products made from wood
grown in sustainable forests. The manufacturing processes conform to the
environmental regulations of the country of origin

ISBN 0 09 944542 5

Photograph Acknowledgements

Laurence Cendrowicz 1; Yvette Cowles 2 (*both*); Express Newspapers 3 (*both*), 4 (*top
right*), 6 (*top*), 8; Sean Smith 4 (*bottom left*); Barry Batchelor/PA Photos 5 (*top*); Jim
Wileman/Apex Photo Agency 5 (*below*); Reuters/ Popperfoto 6 (*below*); Ian
Torrance/Mirror Syndication 7 (*top*); Hugo Philpott/AFPPhoto 7 (*below*).

Four lines from 'Dedicatory Ode' by Hilaire Belloc. Reprinted by permission of PFD
on behalf of: *The Estate of Hilaire Belloc* ©: as printed in the original volume.

Typeset by MATS. Southend-on-Sea, Essex
Printed and bound in Great Britain by
Bookmarque, Croydon, Surrey

Contents

Acknowledgements   vii

Introduction   ix

One: Opening the Chamber   1

Two: A Bookish Child   16

Three: A Rebel in Hiding   49

Four: Goodbye to the Forest   71

Five: Natural Woman   86

Six: Love in a Warm Climate   114

Seven: The Poverty Trap   135

Eight: A Little Bit of Help   151

Nine: The Prime of Miss Joanne Rowling   166

Ten: On the Move   188

Eleven: Public Property   197

Twelve: Hollywood   206

Thirteen: *Honoris Causa*   218

Fourteen: Sweet Charity   234

Fifteen: And the Winner is . . .   240

Sixteen: Fort Knox   247

Seventeen: A New Chapter   258

Afterthoughts   276

Bibliography   283

Acknowledgements

Writing this book would not have been possible without the help of a long list of people. I hope I have remembered them all. There were also those who wanted to remain anonymous and I have respected that. I thank them and hope they will be pleased with the finished result.

Those I would like to especially mention are: Andrea Andrews, Jenny Brown, Professor Keith Cameron, Ken Carruthers, William Clark, Tanya Cowles, Yvette Cowles, Suzie Cross, Barry Cunningham, Ray Davison, Richard Easton, William Ford, Lindsey Fraser, Giles Gordon, Tim Gray, Alan Hall, Helen Hall, Linda Hay, Catherine Jones, Charles Lewis, Sylvia Lewis, Zoë Longbridge-Berry, Matilda Mitchell, John Nettleship, Shirley Nettleship, Dale Neuschwander, Alasdair Paterson, Gillie Peacock, Ian Potter; Ruby Potter; John Powell, Rebecca Rampton, Dai Rees, Nigel Reynolds, Dennis Rice, Geoff Roser, Professor Martin Sorrell, Moira

Stewart, Keith Wheatley, Paula Whitehouse, Eliane Whitelaw and Jared Wilson.

I would like to thank Emilia Saunders and TAP Air Portugal for my travel arrangements to Porto, Steve Cassidy and Maria Inês Aguiar of the Encounter English School for their friendly hospitality while I was there, David Higham Associates for assistance with Elizabeth Goudge, and Yate Heritage Centre.

At Michael O'Mara Books my thanks to Michael O'Mara for commissioning the book, Helen Cumberbatch for her tireless work as editor, Gabrielle Mander and Toby Buchan for their wise advice and Judith Palmer for her picture research. Special thanks to Bryony Evens for her enthusiasm and help.

I am also grateful to Zoë Lawrence for her help with the manuscript.

My final thank you is to J. K. Rowling for being an inspiration.

Introduction

HARRY POTTER HAD passed me by. It was October 2000 and the books about the schoolboy wizard had been on the shelves of every bookshop and in almost every home for three years. But not my own.

I had seen Thomas Taylor's famous illustration for the first book on countless displays and vaguely wondered if he was imagining a young John Lennon or even Elvis Costello when he drew it. I had also cast an envious eye over the bestsellers' list in the Sunday newspapers and found that Harry Potter week after week was easily outstripping Jeffrey Archer, Joanna Trollope, Nick Hornby and the usual suspects. I even toyed with the idea of writing a collection of stories about a magic cat based on my own puss who sits on my lap snoring while I tap away at my computer. But that was the extent of the impact Harry Potter had made on my life. And I had absolutely no idea who J. K. Rowling was. I guessed it was a pseudonym, probably for a kindly aunt tending roses in a Surrey garden.

All this was to change as I read the *Sun* newspaper over a morning cappuccino in my local café in West London. Page one of the *Sun Woman* supplement – essential reading for the man about town – was given over to 'My Life as a Lone Parent', a 2000-word article by Harry Potter author J. K. Rowling. I read it from start to finish. It began by declaring that Joanne Rowling was Britain's highest paid woman, earning more than £20 million ($30 million) in the previous year. Yet just six years before she had been a newly divorced mother of a young baby, caught in a benefits trap, stuck in poor housing and unable to improve her situation without endangering the essential payments needed to live.

The author described how the breakdown of her marriage led her to the social security office in Edinburgh on a snowy December day: 'I realized I was about to start living on £70 ($105) a week – £70 to feed and clothe myself and my baby daughter and to pay all our bills.' Joanne, then twenty-seven, was luckier than some. She could afford the deposit on a rented flat, one bedroom with a living room and kitchen combined. 'The best you could say about the place was that it had a roof,' she recalled. 'If I concentrated hard enough maybe I'd be able to block out the sounds of mice behind the skirting board.'

There was to be no easy solution, no shout of 'eureka!' as the first words of Harry Potter gold tumbled onto a page. The door to better accommodation was effectively closed by a policy of non-rental to people on housing benefits. To make matters worse she could sensibly work only two hours a week as a secretary because any pay exceeding £15 ($22.50) a week was deducted directly from benefit. Bureaucracy, it seemed, was determined that those caught in the poverty trap should stay there. And presiding over this social injustice was the prime minister, John Major, who infamously declared that the breakdown in discipline among modern children was the fault of single parents.

Two things from the article tweaked my emotions. First was Joanne's description of going to the post office for the first time to collect her income support: 'I felt as though there was an enormous neon arrow pointing at my head. I got out my benefit book only when I reached the counter and handed it over quickly hoping nobody would notice what it was.' The second was the gift of used and worn toys brought round by a well-meaning health visitor for her daughter. They included a grubby old teddy bear which Joanne refused to give to Jessica: 'If I'd felt humiliated before, it was nothing to how I felt when I looked at that teddy bear.'

Joanne Rowling was lucky. She had friends who would help her financially to drag herself away from the benefit stranglehold and she was able to train as a teacher. If the Harry Potter phenomenon had not come along just after she qualified, she would still have escaped the stigma of single motherhood by determination and hard work: 'To say that most single mothers aren't that lucky is a wild understatement. Six out of ten British families headed by a single parent are living in poverty.'

The purpose of the *Sun* article was to alert and inform people about what is happening in Britain today, revealing how society is divided not, as has been the case in the past, by class and the accident of one's birth, but by money. Through the article Rowling was publicizing her role as an ambassador for the newly formed National Council for One Parent Families. This struck me as a responsible and refreshing use of fame and celebrity. I decided to learn more about her.

I did not have long to wait. One Sunday morning I turned on my radio to discover her telling Sue Lawley her choice of *Desert Island Discs*. Her music selection was interesting in its honesty – 'Everybody Hurts' by REM, for instance, reflecting her misery that first Christmas in Edinburgh when she faced the social security offices for the first time. But more interesting was what she revealed about her life between the records. Her mother had suffered from a 'galloping' form of multiple sclerosis diagnosed when Joanne was fifteen. 'Home,' she admitted 'was a difficult place to be' Joanne's mother had subsequently died at forty-five.

For those who like lists – and I am one of them – her choice of records was: The Beatles – 'Come

Together', The Smiths – 'Bigmouth Strikes Again', Beethoven – *Appassionata* Sonata, Tchaikovsky – Violin Concerto in D Major, REM – 'Everybody Hurts', Marianne Faithfull – 'Guilt', Jimi Hendrix – 'All Along the Watchtower' and Mozart – Requiem Mass in D Minor, which was her favourite of all. Rowling came across as modest, thoughtful and easy to talk to. I was intrigued that when she listened to the *Appassionata* she imagined herself on stage in a ball gown playing the piece before an enthralled audience. She hardly needed to admit to a 'rich fantasy life'.

Here then, from two sources, was a sketchy life story that was more like a work of fiction in which a young heroine faces all manner of difficulties and sadness before her final triumph over adversity. The time had come for some proper research. My first port of call was the internet where I came across an article entitled *The Not Especially Fascinating Life So Far of J. K. Rowling.* Surely some mistake. If ever there was a life both dramatic and colourful, then this was it. She may not have fought in the trenches of the First World War or discovered a cure for smallpox but, in terms of human emotion and the power of imagination, then Joanne's thirty-five years were going to take some beating. The standard media biography hardly did her justice but at least it divided her life into easy sections: born in Chipping Sodbury, lived in Bristol until the age of nine, moved to village near Chepstow, comprehensive school, Exeter

University, death of mother, move to Portugal to teach English, marriage and daughter, return to Britain, Harry Potter.

What can I say about Harry Potter? I bought the first four books at once and read them so rapidly that I was disappointed when I had nothing left to read. Much has been made of Harry Potter's accessibility to adults. Most classic children's stories can be read over and over again throughout one's life. I still love to read *The Wind in the Willows* by Kenneth Grahame and the *William* books of Richmal Crompton, whose delicious irony escaped me when I first read them at the age of seven. That I suppose is the secret of longevity in works of children's fiction – as we get older, wiser perhaps, we discover different things in the books. A ten-year-old reading Harry Potter may enjoy the good old-fashioned battle of hero versus villain and the wonderful imagination of it all. I found Harry a tormented character, unexpectedly given the power to change the course of his unpromising life.

My resolve in this book was to trace the footsteps of Joanne Rowling in the hope perhaps of discovering the influences that gave birth to Harry Potter, Hermione, Ron, Hagrid, Snape et al. I wanted to find out who Harry Potter is. It promised to be a fascinating journey. His creator had told Sue Lawley that newspaper articles about her were 50 per cent fact and 50 per cent embroidery. I had a feeling that J. K. Rowling, the person, was more interesting than Harry Potter, the fictional hero.

INTRODUCTION

Joanne's entry in *Who's Who* was far from helpful and at just 111 words, of which a mere forty were biographical, did little to fill in the gaps in the J. K. Rowling story. There was no mention of where she was born or where she went to school. Reference was made to her marriage in 1992 but her subsequent divorce was ignored. There was obviously a great deal to do. At least I knew where to start: Chipping Sodbury. The only problem was, I discovered, that J. K. Rowling was not actually born in Chipping Sodbury and never lived there . . .

CHAPTER ONE

Opening the Chamber

'Joanne's upstairs doing her writing.'

MR AND MRS ROWLING, of number 109, Sundridge Park, were proud to say they were perfectly normal, thank you very much. This was their first home as newly-weds, fresh faces from London starting out on an adventure with a baby soon to be born. It had all happened very quickly for the young couple who had met just over a year before on a train from King's Cross station taking them some 500 miles north to their naval posting at 45 Commando, Arbroath, on the east coast of Scotland. The train had old-fashioned compartments and fate lent a hand when the short, dark-haired recruit with a Cliff Richard quiff squeezed into the seat next to the pretty Wren. In those days of the early sixties it was a journey of nine hours to central Scotland and afforded the two eighteen-year-olds plenty of time to get to know each other. They snuggled up together underneath Pete's duffel coat and watched the countryside roll by.

Over the following months their relationship

blossomed and Pete Rowling and Anne Volant decided that a life at sea was not for them. Anne had fallen pregnant which, in terms of the armed services and society as a whole, was a bigger deal in 1964 than it is today. They chose to follow the example of Pete's father Ernie and try their luck away from London, as they both wanted a rural upbringing for their child. Ernie had moved from Walthamstow, an unprepossessing borough of north-east London most famous for its greyhound track, to the village of West Moors, not far from Bournemouth, where he opened a grocery shop which would later be a source of inspiration for his granddaughter Joanne.

Ernie had been a machine-tool setter by trade and Pete decided again to follow his father's path and look for work in the engineering industry. He secured a job as an apprentice on the production line at the Bristol Siddeley factory at Filton, a district of Bristol. It would be a chance to put down roots in the West Country. But first there was the little matter of getting married.

All Saints Parish Church was close to Anne's parents' home in Fairmead Road, Tufnell Park, then a far from fashionable area of north London. The invasion of young professionals, which would turn the countless rows of large terraced houses into desirable and therefore expensive residences, was twenty years and more into the future. All Saints in Tytherton Road was a Victorian monstrosity of 1884, so large it could have comfortably held two or three weddings at the same time without any of the parties bumping into one another. Typically it has been deconsecrated now and turned into eight luxury flats each with a separate entrance dotted around its imposing structure.

By the time of the wedding on 14 March 1965 Anne was five months pregnant, more than a little noticeable on her petite frame. It was two weeks after her new husband's twentieth birthday and just six weeks after her own. They were very young to be starting out with a baby on the way and could easily have slipped into depressing London bedsit life, but Pete's dynamism and industry ensured that would not happen to his family, however young they were.

Such responsibilities on a couple barely out of their teenage years meant the 'swinging sixties' passed them by. History, or more precisely nostalgia, tends to forget that the sixties were only a generational blink away from the Second World War. Both Anne and Pete were conceived in wartime and brought up in a country where recovery from the ravages of six years of conflict was slow. When they married, a young Welshman called Tom Jones was number one in the pop charts with 'It's Not Unusual'. His booming voice would soon be replaced by the bad boys of the music scene the Rolling Stones with 'The Last Time'. Joanne Rowling later recalled that her parents both loved The Beatles and had all their LPs and would dance

3

around the living room to their music. It was a reminder of their youth before they became an old married couple at twenty. By no stretch of the imagination could Yate, where they set up home, be described as swinging.

Yate, ten miles north-east of Bristol, the largest city in the West Country, is a sprawling 'new town'. These modern creations are traditionally condemned as having no heart, no soul and no sense of community. In 1965 Yate's worst days of housing and industrial estates mushrooming out from a shopping-mall epicentre were all ahead of it. It had a distinctly rural flavour when Pete and Anne moved into their modest single-storey first home. Sundridge Park was a road surrounded by fields. The only blot on the landscape was 300 yards away at the end of the road where Yate Town Shopping Centre had opened the previous year. It had been fanfared as the first out-of-town shopping centre in the United Kingdom and was aimed at attracting shoppers from Bristol. Like the town itself the centre has grown mercilessly over the years to more than a hundred shops today.

J. K. Rowling has often said that she hails from Chipping Sodbury, a source of inspiration for her love of peculiar names. Chipping Sodbury is Yate's elegant neighbour, brimming with antique shops and quaint hostelries. It has snob appeal and for estate agents a Chipping Sodbury postal address is worth much gold. Yate, however, despite its modern persona, dates back more than two thousand years. The name is a corruption of the Saxon word Gete, Geate or Giete which meant a gateway – in this case to a forested area which was a royal hunting reserve. Local historians have traced the history of the Manor of Yate from a Saxon charter of *c.* AD 778 in which Offa, king of Mercia, confirmed a grant of ten 'mansiones' in Gete to Worcester Abbey.

During the Second World War Yate was targeted by the Germans because of the Parnall Aircraft factory in the town. German war archives reveal that Yate was photographed by a Nazi reconnaissance plane five days before war was declared on 3 September 1939. The following February a single German bomber flew unchallenged over the town and bombed the factory, killing fifty-two of the 4,000 workers inside. Three of the six bombs failed to explode or the death toll would have been even higher. It was an astonishing raid because the plane, clearly displaying a swastika on its fuselage, flew in above the rooftops in broad daylight before dropping its deadly load. The plane then disappeared into low cloud and escaped without trace.

The Cottage Hospital, 240 Station Road, Yate was originally a private home called Melrose House. In 1920 the local War Memorial Fund invested the then considerable sum of £2,000 ($3,000) to found the hospital in memory of those who had lost their lives in the Great War of 1914–18. The dead from nineteen villages are listed on an impressive wooden plaque in the main hall. In 1951 the general medical beds were transferred to Bristol and the Cottage Hospital became exclusively a maternity unit.

It was a popular place. There was none of the conveyor belt mentality of today's maternity service. Mothers-to-be were allowed a ten-day stay and given a list of items to bring: 'For The Mother: 2 night-dresses, dressing gown, slippers, toilet articles, 2 bath towels, 2 brassieres, 1 pkt maternity pads, blood group card, milk token book. For The Baby: powder, soap, safety pins, 2 muslin napkins.' Visiting hours were daily from 7 p.m. to 8.15 p.m., husbands only. At the bottom of the printed instruction sheet was the stern warning, 'Children not allowed'.

Anne Rowling arrived in late July 1965 to take her place in one of the twelve beds under the watchful eye of matron Miss Irene Norton, known

OPENING THE CHAMBER

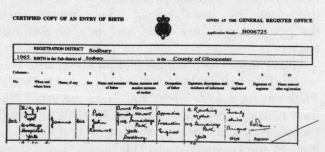

A copy of Joanne Rowling's birth certificate.

affectionately as Nellie. There was a great feeling of camaraderie among the mothers. On 31 July Anne gave birth to a girl described much later by J. K. Rowling herself as 'fat and blonde'. Anne and Pete decided to call her Joanne – that name alone.

Joanne Rowling's earliest memory is of the birth of her sister Dianne. The new addition to the Rowling family was born at home in the main bedroom of number 109, Sundridge Park. It was 28 June 1967. She told Lindsey Fraser in *Telling Tales: An Interview with J. K. Rowling*, 'My dad gave me playdough the day she arrived, to keep me occupied while he ran in and out of the bedroom. I have no memory of seeing the new baby, but I do remember eating the playdough.' Dianne, like her sister and mother, was given just the one forename. Everyone called her Di.

Pete was progressing well at the Bristol Siddeley factory and had finished his apprenticeship. He was a bright young man and was looking to improve things for his wife and young family. Their house in Sundridge Park was already showing signs of being lost in an expanding grey housing estate. It was not the village life the Rowlings had wanted for their daughters.

Four miles away lay Winterbourne; too big to be a village, too small to be a town and now little more than a suburb. Historically it had been a farming and quarrying centre. It had more of a sense of community than Yate and Pete Rowling came across Nicholls Lane, a street of neat three-bedroomed grey stone houses built by a local developer in 1963. They cost £2,999 ($4,499) new and not much more when he made an offer acceptable to Ken and Rowena Evans for number thirty-five. It may not have been their dream home but it was a step in the right direction. Alan Hall, who lived two doors down, recalls, 'This was fields all around when we first came here. Across from the end of the road was an old country garage and a blacksmith's shop. It's a Safeway now.'

Anne and Pete, naturally friendly Londoners, fitted in well in what was essentially a cosmopolitan society with people from all over the country coming together to work at the Bristol factories and settle in the villages and towns nearby. Many worked at Bristol Siddeley which, after a series of takeovers, was merged into a single company, Rolls-Royce, in 1971. Contrary to popular belief the factory, which employed more than ten thousand workers, did not make expensive cars but specialized in aircraft engines. Pete worked in the 'build shops' where the engines were assembled. His particular shop made the Pegasus engines for Harrier fighter planes. It was a hard working day, from 7.30 a.m. to 5 p.m., and often the employees would stay longer, unwilling to leave a job incomplete at the end of their shift. Pete soon began to make his way up the management ladder, moving away from assembly line work.

The Rowlings and Halls became good friends.

All four had been in the armed services – Anne and Pete in the Royal Navy, Alan and Helen Hall in the RAF. Alan also made the half-hour journey to the Bristol Siddeley factory every morning. On a Sunday he and Pete would stroll down to the Wheatsheaf Inn in the High Street for a pint while the wives prepared a traditional Sunday lunch. Alan recalls, 'I always remember the discussions about politics I had with him. Essentially he was a quiet chap who took things seriously and perhaps Joanne gets that from her dad. She certainly looked quite like her dad.'

Nicholls Lane was a neighbourly street. Helen Hall remembers how one year when Anne was ill with pleurisy all her neighbours rallied round to help with shopping and meals and looking after Joanne and Di. On New Year's Eve the Halls would play host to their neighbours. Helen is Scottish and a little touch of Hogmanay would always come to Nicholls Lane and Anne and Pete would pop in, sit on the floor with their friends and welcome in the New Year.

With Pete working long hours, Anne Rowling provided the greatest early influence on their daughters. She had given up her career to be a young mother. Joanne later explained, 'She settled down to raise her family and keep house, and I never saw the faintest sign, later in her life, that she regretted not having enjoyed the single life more.' Anne brought her love of books into the lives of her family and it was here in Nicholls Lane that the first

9

glimmers of J. K. Rowling's unbridled imagination took shape.

Her father provided her first memory of books when he read her *The Wind in the Willows* while she was stuck at home with the measles. Joanne has yet to reveal how she thought up the name of Weasley for Harry Potter's best friend but it does sound rather similar to measly. First books can have a great influence on childhood minds. Pete Rowling would pull up a chair next to the bunk beds in the back bedroom and enthral his four-year-old daughter with the exploits of Rat, Mole, Mr Toad and Badger. Animals are enormously important in the Potter stories, especially in the way they are used to discuss morality and the frailty of human emotions. It is a path well worn in Kenneth Grahame's fantasy. There are elements of Toad, a dreadful show-off full of boastfulness and vanity, in the swaggering Gilderoy Lockhart, teacher of Defence Against the Dark Arts in *Harry Potter and the Chamber of Secrets*. Perhaps Hogwarts' headmaster Dumbledore has a little of Badger in his sensible character. Most strikingly Grahame's Wild Wood and Rowling's Forbidden Forest serve the same purpose of being somewhere dark and threatening for heroes and good folk generally.

Ian Potter, one year younger than Joanne, lived at number twenty-nine. 'When you walked in to the Rowlings' there was cabinet after cabinet of books,' he recalls. His mother Ruby and Anne would swap them. Their favourites were the popular historical romances of the day by authors like Victoria Holt.

Anne would always be reading to her daughters. 'She thought stories were very much part of bringing children up,' says Ruby Potter. The very young Joanne never cared much for the Noddy books of Enid Blyton. The tales of Big Ears, PC Plod, Golliwog and the hero himself, who always wore a pointy hat with a bell on it, failed to fire her imagination. Richard Scarry, however, was a different proposition – another example of how children love animals assuming human characteristics.

The Scarry books, which first appeared in the late 1960s, brilliantly used cats and mice, pigs and dogs and all manner of other animals to inform and educate children about the world. So popular are classics like *Busiest People Ever* and *What Do People Do All Day?* that many new editions have been published in the last couple of years. Trains, which have always been important in the life and work of J. K. Rowling, feature in almost every Scarry book, usually driven by a fox. Her parents met on a train, the idea of Harry Potter was conceived on a train and, in the books themselves, the Hogwarts Express transports Harry from the misery of his real or 'Muggle' world to escape and wizardry.

The young Joanne Rowling loved the Scarry books and they inspired her, at the age of six, to put pen to paper and write her first story. It was called 'Rabbit'. The eponymous hero was stuck at home suffering from the measles and was cheered up by friends who dropped in, including a giant bumblebee called Miss Bee. Joanne has always been fond of rabbits. She had started entertaining her younger sister by making up a story about Di falling down a rabbit hole and being fed strawberries by a family of bunnies. The family terrier was named Thumper after the cheeky rabbit in the Walt Disney film *Bambi*. The young Rowling girls always wanted a rabbit themselves and were jealous of the Potter family who had a black and white one called Flump which the two girls would be forever feeding morsels of grass.

'Rabbit', as Joanne acknowledges, may have been a bit of a rip-off from Richard Scarry – in one of his stories a young rabbit is ill in a hospital bed – but the extraordinary thing was that a six-year-old wanted to spend time making up a story. Helen Hall recalls going round to see Anne and enquiring about her eldest daughter. 'Joanne's upstairs doing her writing,' came the proud reply. What most parents would give to have a child happy in her bedroom reading or writing stories.

The first person to hear Joanne's story was her sister and it has remained that way for thirty years. Di's enthusiasm for this creativity has been one of the great encouragements in the life of J. K. Rowling. Her mother too loved to hear her daughter's stories and the dedication in the first Harry Potter book acknowledges both. This family support gave the young Joanne the confidence and enthusiasm to continue to make up stories and share them with others. Her immense imagination also made her the natural leader of the kids in Nicholls Lane, who were forever playing in one another's gardens. There were no fences between the front gardens of the properties and neighbours could easily drop in for a cup of tea and a chat or, in the case of the children, a game of wizards and witches devised by Joanne Rowling.

There were neither computer games nor mobile phones to preoccupy them. Instead Joanne, Di, Ian Potter and his sister Vikki would raid Anne Rowling's dressing-up box. 'The children were forever pinching the brooms from the garage to use as broomsticks,' recalls Ruby Potter. 'Joanne was always in charge, always the leader.' Joanne thought up a game where the girls would dress up as witches and the boys as wizards, which usually meant just Ian although sometimes another neighbour Christopher White joined in. They would sit under a tree and Joanne would devise spells and pretend she was making up witches' brews of various disgusting ingredients. 'I used to wear my Dad's long coat back to front to look like a wizard,' remembers Ian. 'I think there were a pair of joke specs in the box as well – a bit like Harry's. Joanne would always make up spells and things and stories where we'd all be the characters.' Throughout her life Joanne's friends would remember her making up stories. Athough she remains shy of showing people what she has written, she has never lost the knack of charming her friends with her flights of fancy.

Joanne may have been the leader but Ian Potter got his revenge on a couple of occasions. One afternoon before tea he persuaded Joanne that a fat juicy slug was an appetizing treat. No wonder that, when she was asked after the publication of Harry Potter what animal she would like to turn into, she replied, 'I'd like to be an otter; that's my favourite animal. It would be depressing if I turned out to be a slug or something.' In Chapter Two (The Vanishing Glass) of *Harry Potter and the Philosopher's Stone* she writes ... 'The Dursleys often spoke about Harry like this, as though he was something very nasty that couldn't understand them, like a slug.' In fact the ghastly Dudley Dursley, with his thick fat head, is rather slug-like.

One weekend Ian's father Graham and his Uncle Roger were building a new garage on the side of number twenty-nine and had laid a concrete floor of wet cement. Mischievous Ian managed to cajole Joanne, Di and his sister Vikki to walk all over the cement, making footprints as if they were Hollywood stars outside Graumann's Chinese Theater on Sunset Boulevard. A disgruntled Pete Rowling had to pop over and help his neighbours smooth over the floor. The irony is that in these crazy commercial times the footprint of the young Joanne Rowling would probably now be worth more than the cost of a new garage.

The one thing that Joanne could not stand was

spiders. Ruby Potter remembers the aversion especially because her daughter shares it. Even today, if J. K. Rowling is asked what she hates, she replies, 'spiders'. No wonder then that they loom large in her books where Ron in particular is frightened of them. The whole childhood nightmare is relived in *The Chamber of Secrets* when Ron and Harry are taken to see Aragog in the Forbidden Forest, where they encounter 'Spiders the size of carthorses, eight-eyed, eight-legged, black, hairy, gigantic'. If Joanne Rowling had to face a Boggart, a creature that transforms itself into the shape of what you fear most, she has said it would be a spider like Aragog.

CHAPTER TWO

A Bookish Child

'Joanne was always more serious . . . chin down, looking ahead, a responsible little person.'

WHEN JOANNE CELEBRATED her fifth birthday, in 1970, there was no McDonald's or Burger King to tempt young palates. Instead the children would sit up at the table and Anne or Ruby would serve them jelly and ice cream, sandwiches and fairy cakes. Anne Rowling was an accomplished cook. 'She loved it,' says Ruby. 'There was no such thing as takeaways. For one thing the money wasn't there. We couldn't go into a supermarket and pick up a meal to just put on the table. We had to prepare meals. Anne would always bake cakes for the family. She would prepare the vegetables not put them in a microwave. Everything was so fresh. We would walk up to the local grocery shop Sullivan's and buy our potatoes and vegetables and fruit.

'We didn't live in each other's pockets but we were both mums and we were both at home. Once you had a family then you were at home. It's not like modern-day mums; they are forced to go out to work to keep the wolf from the door.'

Tea round the table was not just a birthday treat for the Rowlings. Anne always insisted the family ate together and, when Pete came home from work, providing he was not doing overtime, Joanne and Di would immediately stop their games and go home for their meal. From the outset Harry Potter would delight in the variety of delicious food laid before the Hogwarts pupils: for his first school meal in *The Philosopher's Stone* he was presented with a vast selection of dishes including 'roast beef, roast chicken, pork chops and lamb chops, sausages, bacon and steak, boiled potatoes, roast potatoes, chips, Yorkshire pudding, peas, carrots, gravy, ketchup.' No pizza, no Whoppers, Big Macs or KFC specials for these children – just good old-fashioned English cooking, just like Joanne's mother used to make. And that was before the 'apple pies, treacle tarts, chocolate eclairs and jam doughnuts, trifles, strawberries, jelly, rice pudding . . .' that followed for dessert.

Two months after her fifth birthday Joanne went to school for the first time. St Michael's Church of England School was in the High Street, a short step from the Wheatsheaf Inn and a five-minute walk from number thirty-five Nicholls Lane. Anne walked with her elder daughter on that first day, as she was to do for most of Joanne's school life even when she was a teenager. Joanne looked smart in her uniform of red top and grey skirt.

William Wilberforce, renowned as the Member of Parliament who began the campaign in 1788 to abolish slavery, visited the rural areas near Bristol in the early part of the nineteenth century and recommended that a school was needed in Winterbourne. As a result in 1813 a grant of one hundred pounds was provided to found St Michael's. The first premises were in the clubroom of the Green Dragon Inn, where the school remained until 1867 when it moved to a building next to the Wheatsheaf Inn. It seems the good gentlemen of Winterbourne needed to have a drink handy when confronted by 300 small boys and girls together. In 1970 the infant school was still in the High Street, where children would stay for two years before moving to junior school in Linden Close. It was still a five-minute walk from Nicholls Lane except they would turn left out of the house instead of right.

From the beginning Joanne loved the school. The building was like a little Victorian chapel with large bay windows. The only drawback was that, when her mother came to collect her for lunch after her first morning, she thought her schooling was finished for ever. She told the author Lindsey Fraser, 'I thought that was it and that I'd done school and wouldn't need to go back.' There is something charmingly reminiscent of Laurie Lee's *Cider with Rosie* in this ingenuousness. The young Laurie is outraged after his first day at the village school because he had not received a promised gift. He tells his sisters: 'They said: "You're Laurie Lee, ain't you? Well, just you sit there for the present." I sat there all day but I never got it. I ain't going back there again!'

St Michael's was old-fashioned village schooling at its best. The present headmaster Ken Carruthers observes, 'There was much more time for them to be children then.'

The headmaster of the junior school where Joanne transferred in September 1972 was Alfred Dunn, who was much respected in the community despite a slight resemblance to the old-time comedian Arthur Askey. Mr Dunn, in his late eighties, has found himself much in demand by television and newspapers who noted his initials were the same as Hogwarts' head Albus Dumbledore and concluded that he must be the blueprint for that august and wise presence in the Harry Potter books. In fact Dumbledore is better looked for in a future headmaster of Joanne Rowling and in her own father.

Mr Dunn presided over a school where English and maths were a priority, in the days before stringent government curricula. He does not remember Joanne. She was one of the youngest in her class, because of her date of birth on the last day of July, and was particularly shy and quiet at school. But like the other boys and girls she loved the maypole, which went up in the playground to celebrate May Day, and the Michaelmas Mop Fair which took place every year on 29 September. Mr Carruthers explains, 'We have a tradition in the school that every child receives an apple on that day as a reward for being well behaved. It's really a bribe.'

Superficially not much has changed at St Michael's over the years. The infant school is now wardened accommodation for old people but the junior school, with hopscotch chalked on the playground concrete, is still helter-skelter with children rushing around in bright red jumpers, playing their games at break, then fearful of being late for lessons after the old school bell has rung. It is still the same cloche-shaped brass bell, engraved with 'A.R.P.' (for 'Air Raid Precautions'), which brought Joanne scurrying in from the Rec, the grassy expanse of recreation field she walked around every morning with Di and her mother on their way from Nicholls Lane to Linden Close.

Winterbourne was a gentle place. Anne Rowling would often wait with Ruby Potter at the top of Nicholls Lane for their children to emerge after school, her two daughters always hand in hand. The children would be taken to see the ducks on the pond in the centre of the village, or there were the horses and donkeys at the riding stables or sometimes a visit to the docks to see the great ships come in. Anne and Pete Rowling were pleased to be able to give their daughters an old-fashioned childhood in a protected environment. That idyll was about to change for Joanne when she came under the stern eye of Mrs Sylvia Morgan at her next primary school.

Trying to link events and people from Joanne Rowling's life to events and people in the Harry Potter saga is an amusing diversion. Aspects of Mrs

Morgan's fearsome character are embodied in the Hogwarts' Potions master, Professor Severus Snape. Other sources of inspiration are more obvious. Dursley, for instance, an innocuous Gloucestershire town, is saddled with being the surname of the ghastly relations who bring Harry up as an outsider in the 'Muggle' world, forced to sleep in the cupboard under the stairs. A glance at a British gazetteer would reveal Dudley, a town in the West Midlands, on the same page. And there it is: Dudley Dursley, the name of one of the great characters of children's literature without any redeeming characteristics whatsoever.

Dudley is very black and white. The origins of the bespectacled schoolboy Harry Potter are less clear-cut. Perhaps inevitably a myth grew that he was inspired by her childhood friend Ian Potter from Nicholls Lane, Winterbourne. Newspapers desperately wanted to make a simple connection and descended upon him to discover the 'real life inspiration for Harry Potter'. There is no connection beyond the surname. Ian, a family man who lives and works in Yate, is proud to have known Joanne, while she freely admits that the name Potter came from the family who lived a couple of doors down. It might just as easily have come from Dennis Potter, the most famous author of the Forest of Dean where the Rowlings were to move.

When the Harry Potter books first appeared, Ruby Potter wrote to the author congratulating her on her success. A reply arrived 'by owl post', written in Joanne's hand, thanking Ruby for the letter and assuring her that Harry was not based on her son, Ian. Joanne also acknowledged that she 'stole' the Potter surname, which she much preferred to Rowling, a name she hated.

The Potters and Rowlings had ceased being neighbours in 1974 when Pete and Anne fell in love with a village and cottage across the Severn Bridge. For nine-year-old Joanne this new playground was seventh heaven. Just off the B4228 road between the villages of Tutshill and St Briavels is a cliff looking down on the most breathtaking view of the River Wye meandering below. One of many local legends declares that during the English Civil War Sir John Wynters leapt off this cliff aboard his charger and cleared the width of the estuary to escape Cromwell's troops. The Wye here is known as Horseshoe Bend and sweeps past the ruin of Lancaut Church where Joanne would join her fellow Brownies for picnics on warm summer evenings and watch the ravens and buzzards circling above. It is very easy to imagine a young girl's imagination soaring with the birds. Flying, she has said, was a childhood fantasy she was able to incorporate into the Harry Potter series.

To reach a good spot for their feast the Second Tidenham (St Mary's) Brownie Pack would walk from the road past Offa's Dyke – now a trail popular with ramblers – past Spittal Meend, which was once a leper colony, and through the woods, alive with birds singing. For young adventurers it was exciting and enchanting.

Farther on are Otter Hole Caves, miles of labyrinthine passages running under Chepstow racecourse, and on to St Arvans. In *Harry Potter and the Prisoner of Azkaban* Harry, armed with the Marauder's Map, finds his way underground from Hogwarts to the Utopian village of Hogsmeade, by wandering along meandering passageways that seem like a giant rabbit's burrow.

Tutshill, quiet and unspoilt by the passage of time, was gateway to a thousand treasures and secrets for imaginative young minds. Pete and Anne Rowling discovered the village when they travelled across the Severn Bridge and drove on past the border town of Chepstow and up into the Forest of Dean. The bridge, opened by the Queen in 1966, had made this wonderful countryside readily accessible for commuters to Bristol and the journey to the Rolls-Royce factory in Filton was no more than half an hour. When the Rowlings came across a quirky stone-built cottage for sale on the edge of the village they decided it was time to leave Winterbourne.

The sale of their house in Nicholls Lane could not have been easier. A young couple called Tanya and Dave Cowles were looking around the area after spotting some donkeys in a field. They saw a 'For Sale' sign in the front drive of number thirty-five and knew it was the place for them. Tanya remembers that Anne was doing the vacuuming when they first looked in. She was pleased to show them round what was clearly a happy family home with a selection of bicycles in the utility room. Anne was proud of her garden and gave Tanya a pot plant containing white violets. Tanya, also a keen gardener, can still point to two shrubs in the garden which were planted more than twenty-five years ago by Anne Rowling – a staghorn fern and a pink weigela. The Cowles offered £11,000 ($16,500) for the three-bedroomed house which Pete Rowling accepted, keen to move quickly.

For the Rowling sisters, just nine and seven, it was the biggest upheaval of their young lives. It would mean making new friends, settling into a different house and, perhaps most importantly, venturing to a new school. One of the principal reasons why their father chose to uproot his family from a perfectly pleasant but unspectacular home in Winterbourne was Church Cottage itself. Whereas Nicholls Lane was built in 1963, Church Cottage had a long history as well as fantastic views to the Severn Estuary. A unique feature of Tutshill is its position between the Wye and the Severn, wedged in the confluence of the two great rivers. The village is right on the border between England and Wales. Chepstow is just a steep mile away, downhill, in Wales while Tutshill is in the English county of Gloucestershire even though there is a strong Welsh influence in the village.

Despite its striking views Tutshill is hardly a

picture postcard village, stretching too thinly along the main road. It was staunchly middle class. Dai Rees, headmaster of the village school from 1971 to 1991, confirms, 'Tutshill was an upmarket village for the area.' The M4 motorway is ten minutes away but Tutshill retains a feeling of remoteness, standing so close to the inspiring Forest of Dean, 30,000 acres of ancient oaks, beeches and conifers, steeped in myths and legends.

Church Cottage is immediately next to St Luke's Church, on the other side of which is Tutshill Church of England School where Joanne would continue her education. The cottage had the distinction of being the site of the first schoolroom in September 1848 and, until the church was consecrated in 1853, it also held the services of worship in the village, seating a congregation of 120. The cottage continued to be the main school building until 1893 when it had obviously become too small to house the one hundred local boys and girls.

Originally the school was to be for the poor of the parish of Tidenham. The building itself cost £250 ($375) and was paid for by local subscriptions and by sales of theological tracts written by the vicar, the Rev. John Armstrong. Local records show that the annual cost of running the school, including the salary of the schoolmistress, was £30 ($45), which was paid for by subscriptions, the vicar, a contribution called 'school pence', which was one old penny a week per pupil, and a donation from an anonymous person who 'sends it a distance.'

The 1880 Education Act made school compulsory to the age of ten when children could leave, providing they had enough attendances marked in the school log, presumably to start work in local industry. If they did not have sufficient attendances they had to stay until thirteen. Christine Leighton, in her history of the school, reveals that the biggest reasons for non-attendance in this rural backwater were the weather and illness. The children would also miss school for haymaking, potato planting and digging, apple-picking and going to the annual Chepstow Wool Fair in June. They also had the day off to attend the wedding of their needlework mistress, Miss Maggie Evans of Tutshill Lodge, who married on 12 May 1885 and walked up the church path on a carpet of flowers especially prepared by the children.

Church Cottage may have been a little too close to school for the liking of Joanne and Di Rowling but their father was brimming with enthusiasm. Alan Hall, their old neighbour from Nicholls Lane, remembers going to the housewarming party and being given a guided tour by Pete who was anxious to share his plans: 'He had been looking for something that needed doing up. He was so excited about the things he was going to do and was looking forward to it.'

Until moving to Tutshill the Rowlings had lived in modern homes which needed little improvement. Church Cottage, with its flagstone floors, gave Pete the opportunity he was seeking, a chance to blend old features with new ideas. One friend recalls that the first time they saw a gas fire with 'pretend' flames was in the Rowling home. Another visitor was more impressed when Pete rolled back the carpet in the living room to reveal an ancient covered well.

Joanne Rowling walked the twenty yards from the front door of Church Cottage through the kissing gate at the entrance to the playground of Tutshill Church of England Primary School on the first day of the autumn term of 1974. If she had turned around to look past the school's blue railings, she could have seen green fields stretching down to the River Severn and freedom. Inevitably the new girls and boys stood out in their pristine uniforms. Joanne in Cambridge blue blouse, Oxford blue cardigan and skirt was extremely self-conscious and nervous as she made her way into the dingy classroom of Mrs Sylvia Morgan. She was later to describe it as 'pretty Dickensian'. The wooden desks had old-fashioned roll tops with inkwells.

Mrs Morgan struck fear into the hearts of the children of Tutshill. She was by common consent a disciplinarian of the old school. Dai Rees remembers having to reassure parents whose children were about to reach Year Nine, the class of Mrs Morgan: 'The children were in great awe of her and, in some cases, in sheer trepidation. I have had parents complain to me that their children were so terrified at moving in to her class that there would be tantrums and cries and the worried parents would come and see me. I would say to them, "Look, this is something the children may feel now but wait until they are in her classroom. When they have been in her class for some time, they will have got used to her and recognized what a jolly good teacher she was." However much fear they had to put up with, they would appreciate the efforts she made on their behalf. She insisted on standards and wouldn't drop them, which was an exceptionally good thing.' That glowing testimonial for Mrs Morgan, an old-fashioned, Welsh, God-fearing battleaxe would have been no consolation to the small, slightly timid Joanne Rowling.

A fellow pupil describes Mrs Morgan as 'short and full figured, with a weathered face which tended to scowl most of the time. She spent a great deal of her time muttering "tup" when she disapproved of something, which was most of the time. I don't remember anyone actually liking her. People were really scared of her.'

The first thing Mrs Morgan did with a new class of 35–40 boys and girls was to sort out the clever pupils from those who were less able. She did this with an arithmetic test that she called the 'Daily Ten'. It required a degree of mental arithmetic and, on this particular first morning, some knowledge of fractions, which Joanne Rowling had not yet learnt. At least the ordeal was to prove useful when she wrote the chapter called 'The Sorting Hat' in the first Harry Potter adventure. Harry was mortified at the prospect of a test on his arrival at Hogwarts, as he had yet to learn any magic and could not imagine what questions he might have to answer. Fortunately Harry's 'test' turned out to be less of a trauma than he had first feared.

In her own test Joanne scored half a mark, which was rather apt, and was assigned a seat to the far right of the classroom. She did not know it at the time but Mrs Morgan had put her in dunces' row. Joanne did not cry in class. Nor would she cry when she herself became a teacher years later. It would take a despair far greater than that inflicted by this fearsome pedagogue to drive her to tears twenty years on in her story.

For now she applied herself to improving Mrs Morgan's opinion of her abilities. Besides the 'Daily Ten', there were weekly tests affording an opportunity to shine in areas other than maths. Dai Rees recalls, 'Mrs Morgan's strengths were English and she was also excellent in needlework and craftwork. She took all the girlish activities in the school.' Mrs Morgan's philosophy of education was based on the three Rs – reading, 'riting and 'rithmetic – although more than one observer of her methods thought it was more a case of 'repetition, repetition, repetition'. Even the loyal Mr Rees admits, 'You can browbeat children to get their tables learnt. But they become parrot fashion to some extent and the application of them becomes somewhat problematical.'

By the end of the school year Joanne had

graduated to the left-hand side of the classroom for brighter pupils. 'She was clearly well above average ability,' observes Mr Rees. Eventually Mrs Morgan realized this as well. Joanne later recalled, 'I was promoted to second left. But the promotion was at a cost. Mrs Morgan made me swap seats with my then best friend. So in one short walk across the room I became clever but unpopular.'

Although Mrs Morgan had no saving graces in Joanne's eyes, she did come in useful in creating the teaching staff of Hogwarts School of Witchcraft and Wizardry: 'There are a number of people who influenced the character of Snape in my books, and that teacher was definitely one of them. I found her extremely scary.' The chemistry teacher at Joanne's senior school would later lay claim to the dubious honour of being the role model for the Hogwarts' Potions master. Mrs Morgan's influence can also be detected in the character of the deputy head, Professor McGonagall who, in *Harry Potter and the Philosopher's Stone*, tells her pupils, 'Anyone messing around in my class will leave and not come back. You have been warned.'

The relief children felt at having negotiated Mrs Morgan's class was tempered by the knowledge that the following year they would come under the regime of her husband John, the deputy headmaster since 1952. He was tall, avuncular and getting on in years when Joanne moved into Year Ten. One pupil, who remembers him always wearing a pale grey suit, acknowledges, 'He was really quite personable and rarely frightening.'

John Morgan, like his wife, was religious and for many years was a churchwarden in Tutshill. He was also strict and old-fashioned in his methods but was much more popular than his wife. Dai Rees says, 'He was not so regimental. He was still of the old school but not as harsh as his wife. The children liked him.' Another of the teachers at Tutshill, Mrs Nicky Ford recalls, 'Mrs Morgan terrified them all but John Morgan was a super man. After lunch the children used to form two lines in the playground for him to walk back through like a guard of honour.'

Sylvia Morgan died in 1989 and her husband followed her in 1998. She can no longer defend her teaching style. Some, with a misplaced sense of nostalgia, might miss their old-fashioned methods, which were probably better suited to raising the standard of the lowest level in class than developing the special talents of individual pupils. Away from the school the Morgans were pillars of the community. Their friend Sylvia Lewis, who ran the Brownie pack observes, 'They were always good company. They were hospitable and friendly and happy to join in everything. Our daughters and their daughter were friends and I can remember we all used to have fireworks together – that sort of friendly gathering. But Sylvia was a proper schoolma'am and that came first.'

She would barely have recognized the Tutshill School of 2001. Her old drab classroom has been specially painted by parents so that in the words of the present head Linda Hay, 'it's a nicer room to be in'. There is a happy feel to the place, blessed with its outstanding views and basking in the glory of regularly being close to the top of the primary school league in Gloucestershire. Fittingly, in view of the importance of owls in the Harry Potter stories, the school was holder of the Barn Owl Trophy in 2000, a nature quiz competition organized by the Gloucestershire Wildlife Trust in which, coincidentally, Dursley Church of England School finished second.

The older pupils now read to the younger boys and girls and Harry Potter books are the most popular stories for practising these skills. Such is the school's social conscience that it raises money for Comic Relief and Children In Need, has collected more than a thousand pounds for an incubator at a Lithuanian Hospital and sponsors a Ugandan child. Sadly Joanne's memories are clouded by her ordeal at the hands of Mrs Morgan and Tutshill ranks far below her first school in Winterbourne which she loved.

When Tutshill School celebrated its 150th anniversary in 1998, the governors tried to persuade her to help them mark the occasion by launching her third book *Harry Potter and the Prisoner of Azkaban* from there. Not only was she a former pupil, they reasoned, but she also had a strong connection through living for many years at Church Cottage. They were not successful and

Tutshill does not warrant a mention in Joanne's *Who's Who* entry either. It would appear that the acclaimed writer is not given to rash bouts of sentimentality.

In fact the only starring role that Tutshill has in the J. K. Rowling canon is in the Comic Relief booklet *Quidditch Through The Ages* by Kennilworthy Whisp, in which the Tutshill Tornados feature in the list of the Quidditch teams of Great Britain and Ireland. In a small acknowledgement of her old primary school the Tornados wear 'sky blue robes with a double T in dark blue on the chest and back'.

Joanne had her first experience of a death in the family – other than her guinea pigs which were eaten by a fox – when she was nine and her grandmother Kathleen, her father Pete's mother, died in hospital in Poole, Dorset, after a heart attack. She was only fifty-two and Joanne was distraught: 'I adored her and my saddest memory of that time is of her death.' She paid a personal tribute to her grandmother when she adopted Kathleen's name to represent the letter K in the famous 'J. K. Rowling'.

Kathleen and her husband Ernie had run a grocery shop called Glenwood Stores in Station Road, West Moors, near Wimborne Minster in Dorset. Joanne and Di loved it when their parents took them for a visit. The Wimbourne Wasps also feature as one of the Quidditch teams of Great Britain and Ireland.

The grandparents lived in a cosy flat above the store but the real treat for the girls was being allowed to play shop. Provided there were no customers, the sisters were able to use all the real food, tins of baked beans, soup and sardines, packets of crisps and all manner of sweets and pretend they were buying and selling. Joanne would be the shopkeeper carefully weighing everything and Di was the exuberant customer. It kept them amused for hours and ensured that their parents could enjoy a bit of peace upstairs. It also meant that they did not spend every minute watching rubbish on television, although Joanne admits to a weakness for cartoons.

Hogwarts School of Witchcraft and Wizardry remains untouched by the modern technology of education. The common room of Gryffindor does not reverberate to the sound of the *Neighbours* theme tune or Jerry Springer breaking up an audience fight. When Hermione Granger, Ron Weasley and Harry Potter want to find a reference to Nicolas Flamel in the school library they do not operate a vast computer database. They peruse volume upon dusty volume. Books, conversation and mealtimes were the three key family influences on Joanne and these are reflected at Hogwarts. Even in his real 'Muggle' world Harry Potter has no interest in football teams or the latest pop sensation.

Joanne's maternal grandparents were Stanley and Frieda Volant. They lived in the same house in

Tufnell Park for more than thirty years until Stanley's death in 1977. Joanne has described it as a 'shambolic home' and Stanley and Frieda as 'unhappily married'. Certainly she had little affection for Frieda, who preferred her motley collection of dogs to young children and was partly the inspiration for the dreadful Aunt Marge who descends on the Dursley household in *Harry Potter and the Prisoner of Azkaban.* Aunt Marge has plenty of canine wisdom to impart: 'It's one of the basic rules of breeding. You see it all the time with dogs. If there is something wrong with the bitch, there'll be something wrong with the pup'. Joanne has not revealed if grandmother Frieda ever criticized Pete and Anne although the scene where Harry blows Marge up like a balloon is one written with great relish.

Stanley and Ernie, however, are both remembered fondly. Joanne told Lindsey Fraser in *Telling Tales: An Interview with J. K. Rowling* that, 'they were both great characters'. Stanley was a consultant engineer, although in later years he worked as a hospital postman to keep himself busy. 'He was a great dreamer and spent a lot of time in the garden shed, making things,' recalled Joanne. A tribute to her grandfathers can also be found in *The Prisoner of Azkaban* in which Stan and Ernie are the drivers of the Knight Bus that rescues Harry Potter.

Not everything was doom and gloom in Tutshill for the Rowling girls. They loved the Brownies, although Di threw herself into the Tuesday evening gathering with a great deal more gusto than her sister. Sylvia Lewis, Brown Owl, recalls, 'Di was always falling over herself with enthusiasm. She would tumble in, always laughing and she just couldn't wait for us to start. Joanne was always more serious, head down under her little beret, chin down, looking ahead, a responsible little person, you know. They were different characters those girls.' The Tutshill head Dai Rees also remembers Di, with her jet black hair, as being by far the 'livelier of the two girls'.

Joanne was enrolled by Mrs Lewis in the Second Tidenham (St Mary's) Brownie Pack in September 1975. The Enrolment Test consisted of four tasks:

1. Understand: The Brownie Promise (I promise to do my best, to do my duty to God, and the Queen; to help other people every day, especially those at home.); The Law (A Brownie gives in to older folk; a Brownie does not give in to herself.); The Motto (Lend a hand); The Salute; The Smile; The Good Turn; The Brownie Ring; The Pow Wow Ring.
2. Fold and tie her own tie.
3. Plait.
4. Wash up the tea things.

The most difficult of these tasks is folding and tying the tie. It is also the most important. Mrs Lewis explains, 'They had to be able to take it off if anyone broke their arm and use it as a sling. They couldn't become enrolled until they could tie that tie. It was quite complicated for little girls of seven to try and fold up this tie in the right way.' At ten Joanne was more than up to the job. She took three badges while she was in the Brownies: signalling, semaphore and first-aid. Her mother Anne gave her thirty-five pence so she could buy her first-aid book from Mrs Lewis.

The Brownies was good, clean, innocent fun offering a sense of camaraderie and a hint of social responsibility. For about two hours once a week twenty-four girls from the village could get together in the church hall for activities a world away from the steely eye of Mrs Morgan. Joanne joined the others in saving pennies in Smarties tubes. A quarter of a century later she would be celebrating becoming a Triple Smarties Gold Award Winner for children's fiction after receiving the prestigious prize for the third consecutive year in 1999. With the Brownies there were special events to plan for like the Christmas party and Nativity play for the pensioners in the village. The year Joanne joined, the pack was given a special award by the Forest of Dean Round Table for their efforts for the older people in the parish. These were so appreciated that the pensioners returned the favour with a party for the Brownies in a local school. The Brownies also had a Hallowe'en party and a barbecue and, of course, the summer picnics by Lancaut Church.

There is also a definite magical theme surrounding the Brownies. Joanne's pack was divided up into six groups – 'Fairies', 'Pixies', 'Sprites', 'Elves', 'Gnomes' and 'Imps' – names which Joanne may have recalled when she came to write about the elves, Dobby and Winky, and the troublesome gnomes in the Weasleys' garden.

Anne Rowling was one of the youngest mothers in the village and would enthusiastically help with the Brownies and other youth activities. Sylvia Lewis remembers a charity coffee morning at Church Cottage. The Rowlings also allowed the school to use the power from their home for the annual fête and school sports day, never one of the highlights of Joanne's year as she was useless at games. She was a little better at the country dancing which was compulsory at Tutshill School and culminated each summer in the boys and girls giving displays for the village. Truly Tutshill was another world.

Joanne had not deserted the world of books in her new environment. Since her own first effort 'Rabbit' she had written a short story called 'The Seven Cursed Diamonds', although she thought it a novel at the time. The tale of adventure paid more than a little homage to Edith Nesbit, author of *The Railway Children* and *The Story of the Treasure Seekers*. Nesbit was a children's writer with whom the grown-up Joanne would identify more than any other: 'She said that by some lucky chance she remembered exactly how she felt and thought as a child and I would say that I remember vividly what it felt like to be eleven and every age up to twenty and I think you could make a good case just on *The Treasure Seekers* for preventing anybody who doesn't remember what it felt like to be a child from writing a children's book.'

Church Cottage, like their previous home in Winterbourne, was full of books, not least because Anne Rowling's sister was a reader for Mills and Boon and used to send a large box of airy romances every couple of months. Joanne recalled on the BBC Radio 4 programme *With Great Pleasure*, 'I was quite young when I became familiar with the antics of square-jawed, broad-shouldered men in a permanent state of barely controlled arousal and then I'd go back to *What Katy Did* and Enid Blyton and the usual C. S. Lewis.'

'The usual C. S. Lewis' was the classic *Chronicles of Narnia* series, which had an influence on *Harry Potter and the Philosopher's Stone* particularly evident in *The Lion, the Witch and the Wardrobe.* Both novels have a portal that transports the hero or heroine into a fantastical and magical world. In Harry's case it is the inspired Platform Nine and Three-Quarters at King's Cross station. Lewis's heroine was called Lucy and she entered the land of Narnia through a wardrobe and was greeted by a mythological creature, a faun called Mr Tumnus: '"This is the land of Narnia," said the Faun, "where we are now; all that lies between the lamp-post and the great castle of Cair Paravel on the eastern sea.

And you – you have come from the Wild Woods of the West?"

"I – I got in through the wardrobe in the spare room," said Lucy.'

Lewis describes many magical creatures including fauns and one called a boggle as well as a selection of animals that talk, including Aslan the eponymous lion. Mr Tumnus has a collection of books in his bedroom that would not have been out of place in Hogwarts' library: *The Life and Letters of Silenus, Nymphs and Their Ways, Men, Monks and Gamekeepers; a Study in Popular Legend* and *Is Man a Myth?* Lucy's brother Edmund is given a special drink by the evil White Witch: 'It was something he had never tasted before, very sweet and foamy and creamy, and it warmed him right down to his toes.' Harry experiences a similar sensation when he has his first tankard of hot Butterbeer in the Three Broomsticks: 'It was the most delicious thing he'd ever tasted and seemed to heat every bit of him from the inside.'

Joanne has always been candid about the influences of other writers on her work, and is straightforward, honest and self-deprecating about herself as a pre-adolescent girl. She told the radio programme *With Great Pleasure:* 'I was the epitome of a bookish child – short and squat, thick National Health glasses, living in a world of complete daydreams, wrote stories endlessly and occasionally came out of the fog to bully my poor sister and force her to listen to my stories and play the games I'd just invented.' This unflattering and modest appraisal of herself has prompted the obvious observation that she is her own role model for the main female character in the Harry Potter stories, the 'Muggle-born' dentist's daughter Hermione Granger. She does not deny it: 'Hermione was very easy to create because she is based almost entirely on myself at the age of eleven. She is really a caricature of me. Like Hermione I was obsessed with achieving academically, but this masked a huge insecurity. I think it is very common for plain young girls to feel this way.'

Like Joanne, Hermione is a reader of Olympic proportions. At their very first meeting she tells Harry, 'I got a few extra books for background reading, and you're in *Modern Magical History* and *The Rise and Fall of the Dark Arts* and *Great Wizarding Events of the Twentieth Century*.' In *Harry Potter and the Chamber of Secrets* Ron Weasley observes, 'I think she is trying to read the whole library by Christmas.'

Joanne admits, 'I always felt I had to achieve, my hand always had to be the first to go up, I always had to be right.' It is a trait comically shared by Hermione, particularly in the lessons of the dreaded Snape, the Potions master, who regularly ignores Hermione's enthusiastic attempts to attract his attention when she knows the answers to his questions.

Hermione may have a fear of failure but, unlike Joanne, she does not experience it. Whereas Joanne managed a pathetic half a mark in her first taste of Mrs Morgan's 'Daily Ten', Hermione boasts to Harry and Ron that Professor Flitwick, the Charms teacher, told her that she had achieved 112 per cent on his exam. She is naturally top of the year. Intriguingly while Hermione, at least at the beginning of the stories, is little more than a caricature of the know-it-all swot, it is Harry Potter himself who manifests the insecurities of the eleven-year-old schoolgirl who was the real-life Joanne. He is the one filled with dread at the prospect of a test on his arrival at Hogwarts. He is the one who suffers in Snape's classroom just as Joanne would at the hands of her chemistry master John Nettleship at her next school, Wyedean Comprehensive. It is Harry who misses his mother dreadfully, just as Joanne would when her own mother Anne died.

Hermione reveals a deeper, more emotional side to herself towards the end of *The Philosopher's Stone* when she wishes Harry good luck: 'Books! And cleverness! There are more important things – friendship and bravery and – oh Harry – be careful!'

These may be the values of Anne Rowling talking. When Joanne was nine, Anne gave her a book about which she has since candidly admitted: 'Perhaps, more than any other book, it has a direct influence on the Harry Potter books.' It was *The*

Little White Horse by Elizabeth Goudge, which won a Carnegie Medal for children's literature when first published in 1946. It was televised on the BBC under the tide *Moonacre*, presumably to keep the interest of little boys who might not watch something with a soppy tide. On the cover of the 2000 edition there is a quote from J. K. Rowling: 'I absolutely adored *The Little White Horse*. It had a cracking plot . . . It was scary and romantic in parts and had a feisty heroine.'

The Potteresquely named heroine, Maria Merryweather, may be feisty but Joanne Rowling would have identified more with the fact that she was plain and had red hair: 'She was 13 years old and was considered plain, with her queer silvery grey eyes that were so disconcertingly penetrating, her straight reddish hair and thin pale face with its distressing freckles.'

As a template for writing a successful children's novel *The Little White Horse* could scarcely be bettered. Unconsciously the essential components were tucked away in the fertile mind of the young Joanne Rowling ready to serve her well when Harry Potter was taking shape fifteen years and more later. The characters have rich and unusual names. Besides Maria Merryweather there is her governess Miss Heliotrope, Monsieur Cocq de Noir, Loveday Minette and the dwarf Marmaduke Scarlet who, like the house-elf Dobby in the Potter saga, works in the kitchen, cooking and cleaning.

Maria is an orphan and, also like Harry, is thrust

into an unfamiliar world. She travels from London with Miss Heliotrope and Wiggins to her cousin's castle, set in the beautiful and mysterious Moonacre Valley. To reach the castle they must travel through an underground tunnel. The 'character' of Wiggins is a playfulness on the part of Goudge which J. K. Rowling would have appreciated. Wiggins, we are told, is 'greedy, conceited, bad tempered, selfish and lazy'. Why on earth is Maria travelling with him? A page later all is revealed. Wiggins is a pedigree King Charles spaniel.

Animals have a great part to play and, as in the Harry Potter series, they are not always what they seem. Wrolf, a huge tawny dog, turns out to be a lion. He is Maria's protector. Zachariah the cat is very clever and writes hieroglyphic messages with his tail in the ashes in the kitchen hearth. Serena the hare is also wise. In the Harry Potter stories there is a clever cat, Crookshanks, owned by Hermione, who knows that Ron's pet rat Scabbers is really the dastardly Pettigrew in Animagus form.

And then there is the Little White Horse itself galloping through the pine forest: 'She [Maria] was not even surprised when he turned his lovely head a little and looked back at her and she saw a strange little silver horn sticking out of his forehead. Her little white horse was a unicorn.' Harry, too, discovers the mythical creature in the Forbidden Forest: 'Something bright, white was gleaming on the ground. They inched closer. It was the unicorn all right and it was dead. Harry had never seen anything so beautiful and sad.' The unicorn also features in the Comic Relief publication *Fantastic Beasts & Where to Find Them* by Newt Scamander in which we learn it is 'so fleet of foot it is difficult to capture'.

Nowhere can the astonishing influence of Goudge's book on Potter be seen to more striking effect than in the descriptions of food: 'There is sufficient plum cake, saffron cake, cherry cake, iced fairy cakes, éclairs, gingerbread, meringues, sylla-bub, almond fingers, rock cakes, chocolate cakes, parkin, cream horns, Devonshire splits, Cornish pasty, jam sandwiches, lemon curd sandwiches, lettuce sandwiches, cinnamon toast and honey toast to feed twenty and more.' Amazingly that is not a description of a Hogwarts feast but comes from the last chapter of *The Little White Horse*. Refreshingly J. K. Rowling is happy to acknowledge her debt to her favourite childhood book.

Elizabeth de Beauchamp Goudge was born in 1900 into a more genteel world than that of Joanne Rowling in Sundridge Park, Yate, but her desire to write and her modesty in her own achievements bear the closest comparison with the author she would later influence so much. Goudge was half-French, her mother's parents being, so they said, descended from William the Conqueror's cup-bearer. Joanne's own mother Anne, whose maiden name was Volant, also had Gallic ancestry.

Elizabeth's father was principal of the

theological college attached to the cathedral at Wells in Somerset and they lived in an atmospheric old house 'with carved angels in the corners of the room and dark corners and passages that were wonderful for hide-and-seek.' Her mother was an invalid and, according to Elizabeth, was the 'most wonderful storyteller in the world'. There are many aspects of her early life that correlate with Joanne Rowling's but the influence of her mother is the most striking. Although Elizabeth Goudge lived in a far more romantic period in Edwardian England, the modern-day Forest of Dean remains in a time warp.

Elizabeth never went to primary school but her governess Miss Lavington was a stern creature who, if not as frightening as Mrs Morgan with her 'Daily Ten', would 'pound' knowledge into her young charge's brain until she could 'repeat from memory the dates of the Kings of England from William the Conqueror downwards and my tables up to twelve times twelve'. An only child, Elizabeth would spend her afternoons playing with a group of young friends in each other's gardens. Her family holidays were spent on the island of Guernsey where, she recalled, the 'deep water lanes running down to the rocky bays, with their pools of sea anemones, were a paradise for a child'.

When her father became Canon of Ely Cathedral in Cambridgeshire, Elizabeth and her family moved to a haunted house which had been part of the monks' infirmary in the days when there had been a monastery at Ely. 'Nearly every house round the cathedral had its ghost story,' recalled Elizabeth, 'and I saw a grey monk walking about our house so often that I ceased to be frightened of him.'

All these childhood experiences found their way in some form or other into Goudge's novels. She was painfully shy particularly about her English essays. At boarding school her compositions were read aloud to the class 'while I sat with crimson ears sticking out above my pig-tail and modestly lowered head; but secretly bursting with pride'. Her early efforts met with the same fate as would befall J. K. Rowling: they were rejected by the literary world. She supplemented her income by teaching, in her case arts and crafts, and writing when she could: 'I got up early and wrote before breakfast, late at night and in all my odd moments.' She actually burned her first novel because she thought it frightful and her next attempt, *Island Magic* about Guernsey, was turned down by two publishers before finally being accepted by Gerald Duckworth and Co. It is a sequence of events eerily reminiscent of what Joanne Rowling would endure. Almost uncannily they both achieved their first literary success at the age of thirty-two.

At this stage Goudge concentrated on adult novels, culminating in *Green Dolphin Country*, her amazing account of a true story about a Channel Island man who emigrated to the New World and, when he had made his fortune, wrote to the father of the girl he loved and asked for her hand. He had, by misfortune, confused the names of two sisters and throughout the subsequent marriage he never told his wife of his mistake. The most famous of her children's books, *The Little White Horse* and *The Vale of Song*, were written after the Second World War and remain the ones Elizabeth declared she was 'least ashamed of' – a typically modest appraisal.

The parallels between the lives of Elizabeth Goudge and Joanne Rowling are diverting, though not as important as the obvious literary influence the former had on the latter. Both authors possess what the *Dictionary of National Biography* described as 'the fertile imagination of the born storyteller'.

They are not, of course, mirror images of one another. Elizabeth Goudge, a committed Christian, lived her life as a gentlewoman protected from poverty, childbirth and loneliness. She borrowed from her own experiences and wrote about what she knew, producing sixteen novels and six children's books. The endorsement of J. K. Rowling may bring a new generation of recognition.

In *The Little White Horse* the Merryweather motto is, 'The brave soul and the pure spirit shall with a merry and a loving heart inherit the kingdom together'. It is a reminder of Harry Potter's courage and Hermione Granger's enthusiasm for friendship and bravery.

CHAPTER THREE

A Rebel in Hiding

*'There is absolutely nothing
for young people to do.'*

THE TEENAGE GIRLS at Wyedean Comprehensive could be divided loosely into five categories: swots, school tarts, bullies, smellies and the rest, the bunch of ordinary kids who make up the foot soldiers of life. Her contemporaries placed Joanne, or Jo as she now preferred to be called among her friends, firmly in the category of intelligent swot. The image of a Hermione Granger type was one which would take her a few years to shake off but in her early teens Joanne began to change from the 'school spanner' into a more popular, sociable girl whom her schoolmates liked enough to vote head girl in her last year. Joanne has described the honour as being voted the 'least likely to go to jail', which speaks volumes for her opinion of the school. She did concede once that she 'quite liked secondary school' but that is not how one of her friends saw it: 'Wyedean was a dreadful school and you cannot underestimate how much Jo and I could not wait to leave it.'

Joanne began to be more sociable and outgoing as a young teenager. Almost all her contemporaries from Tutshill School went on to Wyedean which, in 1976, was a modern comprehensive, just moved to new premises in the next village of Sedbury. Today the two miles from Church Cottage to the school is so lined by houses that it is difficult to know where one village ends and the other begins. Sedbury is dominated by the sprawling school buildings and, across the other side of Beachley Road, an army barracks. Pupils did not need to pass an exam to enter Wyedean. It was simply a case of being in the catchment area. As a state comprehensive school, there were no fees to pay.

Wyedean is not a school that the government could describe as a 'bog-standard comprehensive'. There is a world of difference between the provincial state school and some of its inner city counterparts in which the comprehensive system has to a great extent emphasized social segregation. The former chemistry master John Nettleship observes, 'We always had a genuine mix of people coming from rural backgrounds.' That mix included children from traditional working-class backgrounds and those from the more geographically mobile families who had moved to the area, as the Rowlings had, because they perceived it as a better environment for their children. These commuters had brought new prosperity.

For Joanne, Wyedean heralded freedom from the Morgans. There was, however, a whole new set of teachers with whom to come to terms. The headmaster was Ken Smith, whom Mr Nettleship describes as a 'real gentleman'. A contemporary of Joanne's recalls him more prosaically as 'a stern man with a cane'. Certainly Mr Nettleship's view is that there is more of Albus Dumbledore, headmaster of Hogwarts, in Ken Smith than might have first been apparent considering that he reintroduced corporal punishment to the school.

'It is intriguing that Dumbledore is probably the best wizard in the world but he doesn't actually assert his powers,' explains Mr Nettleship. 'He lets the chaos go on. Ken Smith was a very modest person and he believed in letting his colleagues sort themselves out. In that way he had the benefit of their individual flair and inspiration but, on the other hand, the school was prone to in-fighting – which is also a feature of Hogwarts.' Mr Nettleship's view of the headmaster is not shared by one of Joanne's friends who asserts, 'I am sure Dumbledore has nothing to do with Smith.'

Joanne, in her role as head girl, would have had a much closer contact with the machinery of the school administration and the job of headmaster than most pupils. She may have included some of her old headmaster's traits in Dumbledore but the Hogwarts' head is a combination of several personalities. If Dumbledore's quiet reasoning may suggest something of Ken Smith, it is not necessarily the case that his character is based solely on headmasters from Joanne's school days.

He probably has more in common with her own father Pete, whom Mr Nettleship describes as being 'very wise'.

The influence of John Nettleship himself as a blueprint for Snape, the Hogwarts' Potions master, is more evident. He is thoughtful, concise, sharp-eyed and with an ability to reach the kernel of a problem that must have alarmed his less confident pupils. 'Stinger', as he was unaffectionately known, is happy, even proud, to be the role model for Harry's schoolmaster tormentor. Chemistry was not a subject in which the artistically minded Joanne Rowling would ever excel but, while she may have forgotten the periodic table, she never forgot the trauma of a Nettleship class. 'I would have this manner or style of singling out one pupil after another to ask a question,' he recalls, 'and I would pick on Joanne because she was one of the more capable pupils in the class.'

Harry is often the focus of Professor Snape's harsh scrutiny, squirming in his seat as he struggles to answer the impossible questions posed by his teacher: '"Potter!" said Snape suddenly. "What would I get if I added powdered root of asphodel to an infusion of wormwood?"' For Potter substitute Rowling and you have a picture of the ordeal the young Joanne faced each time she entered the science block for double chemistry. Nettleship observes, 'I think the lack of confidence that we see in Harry is also something she felt in some aspects of her schooling.'

Nettleship accepts the fact that he might have inspired Snape with good humour: 'I think her characters are quite a clever mix but I do see bits of myself in Snape. At first I fancied myself as Albus Dumbledore. Then, when the reporters started driving up to the house saying, "You're Snape, aren't you?" my wife Shirley said, "I have been trying to conceal this fact from you. I didn't like to tell you." I think I was seen by a lot of the pupils as very severe, especially in the 1970s. It was spare the rod and spoil the child.

'One of the key things to me is that Snape is clearly a person who is as much a problem to himself as he is to other people and by the time we get to the end of the Harry Potter story in Book Seven, seeing as most things get explained along the way, I might pick up a few tips as how to manage the rest of my life more easily. I might turn out good after all.'

John Nettleship was particularly significant to the Rowling family because, as head of the chemistry department, he interviewed Anne when she applied for a job as a laboratory assistant shortly after Di had followed Joanne to Wyedean. At first she was not successful.

'It was my call really,' admits Nettleship. 'My wife Shirley was the chief technician and we were looking for a number two. It came down to a choice between Anne and another woman who had quite a track record as a technician. I regret to say that I felt I had better offer the job to the one with the experience. Shirley was pretty cross with me. She turned out to be pretty awful unfortunately. Fortunately she got fed up with the job after a quite short time and left us. We were able to send for Anne, which was lucky for us because she was absolutely excellent.'

It was the perfect job for Anne, who always enjoyed the company of young people. Since her daughters had outgrown the Brownies she was an enthusiastic helper at Tutshill Youth Club, which would meet at the old church hall. She was an accomplished guitarist and would do her best to pass her talent on to Joanne who, as some young teenagers do, saw herself as a rock goddess and craved to play heavy electric guitar.

Anne, Joanne and Di were more like sisters than mother and daughters. They became a familiar sight in Tutshill making their way to Wyedean in the morning and back after school, when they would call in at the shops to get something for dinner. Top of the list was G. and P. Roser, butchers and grocers, licensed game dealers and purveyors of some of the finest sausages throughout Gloucestershire. 'Joanne was always a very quiet girl when they called in,' recalls Geoff Roser. 'They were a close-knit family and, if it was the weekend, then Dad would come along too. Anne and Pete were a very devoted couple.' In those days the road through Tutshill had more backpackers than cars. The three 'girls' would always fill each other in on the day's gossip as they strolled back from school.

Anne, who had a great sense of humour and invariably saw the funny side of things, told them one day of an exciting episode in the biology lab involving a pretty new teacher and her pet beetles. John Nettleship recalls, 'They were horrible creatures. One day they got out and the teacher, the proud owner of these beetles, took flight, leaving poor Anne to try and sort it out. They were up on the ceiling and all over the place. Fortunately they stayed in the preparation room.' Anne thought it a huge joke and by the time she had told and retold the story throughout the day the two-inch beetles had become six-inch little monsters. When Anne told her daughters about them on the way home they would no doubt have reached colossal proportions. Joanne, who has a magpie memory, storing things away for future literary use, recycled the story in the saga of the Blast-Ended Skrewts which Hagrid unwisely introduced to his Care of Magical Creatures class in *Harry Potter and the Goblet of Fire.* The children were supposed to be taking the explosive creatures for a walk, but the three-foot-long Skrewts, 'a cross between giant scorpions and elongated crabs' were uncontrollable, and the class became scattered over a wide area in their efforts to keep hold of their powerful charges. Anne also supervised the hatching of eggs in rural-science classes, not dragons' eggs, but ducks' and hens'.

Joanne was already impressing her English teachers at Wyedean with her imaginative work.

One who was particularly struck by her creativity was a young American student, Dale Neuschwander, who had crossed the Atlantic for a year to gain experience of teaching in an English state school: 'She was a star pupil during creative writing lessons. I only wish I had kept her A-plus essay entitled 'My Desert Island' which she wrote during a literature unit based on the theme of survival. At the time we were reading books like *Lord of the Flies* by William Golding and *Walkabout* by James Vance Marshall.' Years later, when Joanne was a guest on *Desert Island Discs*, she chose the *SAS Survival Guide* as the book she would take. 'You have given me Shakespeare and The Bible, and literature is great, but I really do want to live . . .'

Mr Neuschwander recalls that, although Joanne participated in class discussions, she preferred to express herself in her writing: 'She seemed confident in her abilities, yet perhaps a little shy at times.' He was also impressed by the teacher who was the most important literary influence on Joanne at this time. Lucy Shepherd was a young twenty-something when Joanne joined Wyedean and she was passionate about women fulfilling their potential in a modern society. 'She truly put her heart into her teaching,' observes Mr Neuschwander, 'and she respected the students by teaching them the fundamental skills they needed as well as by nurturing their creativity and love of learning.

'Lucy had a no-nonsense approach but the children were not afraid of her because they could tell she cared. She was a terrific role model for any aspiring teacher. Her classroom was conducive to serious learning because of her excellent organizational skills and her commitment to getting quality work out of her students. I have no doubt that Lucy had a profound effect on Joanne Rowling.'

John Nettleship also pays tribute to Miss Shepherd: 'Lucy had the highest academic standards. She'd got it in for me because I wasn't very helpful at recommending books. I was always too busy trying to blow things up. The thing about new comprehensives at this period in England was that they tended to attract more inspired teachers because they were looking for somewhere they could try out new things. Lucy was an inspirational person.'

Joanne admits that Miss Shepherd was the only teacher she ever confided in, because she inspired trust, but even she was not aware that her pupil harboured a consuming ambition to be a writer. She did, however, instil in the budding writer a realization that she would not get anywhere without precision and paying attention to structure. In *Telling Tales: An Interview with J. K. Rowling* Joanne explains that her respect for her teacher stemmed from the extraordinary passion Miss Shepherd had for her work. She was a feminist and Joanne had never encountered a woman like her before: 'I remember doodling while she was talking one day and she told me that I was being very rude indeed. I said, "But I'm listening," and she told me that I was still being rude. That really stuck with me.'

Regrettably Lucy Shepherd, a very private person, has retired from teaching, which she did so well, and is now working in a Bristol bookshop. Joanne treasures the letter from her that she received after publication of the first Harry Potter story, telling Joanne that she liked the book.

The adolescent Joanne Rowling was beginning to realize there was more to the world than the narrow confines of Wyedean School. She had her first experience of more exotic climes when she was thirteen, on a school exchange trip to a small town near Lille. 'We were not impressed,' recalls a schoolfriend. 'It was very boring. Jo and I thought it was ironic that of all the beautiful places in France we had to end up in a relatively poor, shabby coal town.' The girls were unimpressed by having to use outdoor toilets with just half-doors for privacy and a trench as the 'facility'.

A popular saying of the Forest of Dean region is 'Blessed is the eye that rests between the Severn and the Wye,' although many of the younger population did not see it this way, and it was more of a case of, 'Bored is the eye'. The most famous of the region's writers before J. K. Rowling was the acclaimed dramatist Dennis Potter, author of *The*

Singing Detective and *Pennies from Heaven*. Unlike Rowling, the aptly named Potter was born and bred in the Forest at Berry Hill near Coleford, about ten miles from Tutshill. His work is perhaps even more influenced by the environment of his childhood than Joanne Rowling's. He always acknowledged his debt to this 'strange and beautiful place'. In his last interview before his death in 1994 Potter described the Forest as 'rather ugly villages in beautiful landscape, a heart-shaped place between two rivers, somehow slightly cut off from the rest of England'.

The youth of Wyedean would empathize with the girl Potter talks to in a Cinderford coffee bar in his memoir *The Changing Forest*. He asks her what she thinks of the place, the Forest. She replies, 'This dump, you mean . . . It's just half-dead, that's what. And lots of mopey old people. Nothing to do. Lot of bloody old miseries round here . . .'

Even Wyedean's long-serving headmaster's secretary Paula Whitehouse concedes, 'There is absolutely nothing for young people to do.' Chepstow, the nearest town to Wyedean and Tutshill, does not even have a cinema. It is one of those provincial towns where groups of boys and girls, too young to drink in pubs, drift about aimlessly, gathering in supermarket car parks to smoke cigarettes and practise on their skateboards.

For young people the whole area is like a large open prison. The Wyedean uniform, an un-flattering combination of brown and yellow, was little better than a prison uniform and was widely loathed. To this day Joanne refuses to have either of those colours in her wardrobe.

The nearest cinema is at Coleford and it was here that Joanne went with her friends to see *Grease*, which became the favourite film of her year. The boys were all John Travolta and the girls Olivia Newton John, although Joanne was beginning to show the radical tendencies which made the more subversive character of Rizzo appealing. Played in the film by Stockard Channing, Rizzo would later become the character which her university friends would associate with the undergraduate Joanne. *Grease*, set in a fifties high school in America, is a million miles away from Wyedean and the only small dose of reality is served up by Rizzo, who hides her vulnerability behind a brash exterior.

John Travolta was popular with Joanne's year at Wyedean but the number one man was Leif Garrett, a curly blond heart-throb who adorned the bedroom walls of impressionable girls across the nation. He had two British hits in 1979: *I Was Made for Dancin'* reached number four on the charts and *Feel the Need* got to number thirty-eight. And that was it for Leif Garrett, soon to be replaced by the next teen sensations or, in the case of Joanne Rowling, by The Clash, the thinking person's punk favourites and generally revered as the best of that genre. Joanne was well aware that her hormones were kicking in. A schoolfriend Andrea Andrews recalls, 'She used to sit and spy on a boy in our year with one of her friends, lusting after him. He was tall for a fifteen-year-old and blond, so quite a few girls liked him.' Joanne herself made the point: 'Just because you've got a good brain doesn't mean you are any better than the next person at keeping your hormones under control.'

As for being 'made for dancin", the opportunities were rare. Andrea remembers, 'There was a youth club in Woodcroft and occasional discos at the Drill Hall in Chepstow. They were the highlight of our lives as you could get alcohol and mix with grown-up sixteen-year-olds. Very rarely there might be a disco in the drama hall at school. And that was it.' Joanne developed a lasting love of discos 'down the drill hall', which she would indulge more fully during her foreign adventure in the future.

The urban youth of today in London and other British cities would be open-mouthed at the sheer lack of facilities for teenagers in this provincial backwater where the only place to meet was in Martin's Coffee Shop or in Gregg's the Bakers. The Live and Let Live, a scruffy but amiable pub on the road between Tutshill and Wyedean, was strictly out of bounds for Joanne. When the family moved from Winterbourne to Tutshill, Pete and Anne rarely went out except for a meal with a few close friends. Geoff Roser, the butcher, observes that he never once saw the Rowlings in a pub the whole time they lived in Tutshill.

Like many intelligent yet shy girls Joanne

immersed herself in the more marginal or radical areas of youth culture; hence her liking for The Clash. Her punk phase had one long-lasting effect: for the next ten years she favoured heavy black eye make-up, the trademark of a gothic look displayed by Siouxsie Sioux of Siouxsie and the Banshees.

Her school contemporaries still remember Joanne mostly as 'quiet and shy'. In the company of her special friends she was more forthcoming and would still entrance them with her stories in which they featured as the heroines. One recalls, 'Jo would entertain us with her brilliant wit and colourful stories. She was very inventive and clever at reading tarot cards and palms and weaving a story around it which was pure make believe but had us alternately gripped and then laughing. Her dry and ironic delivery is instantly recognizable in the books. She may have come out of her shell as she grew up but the storyteller was always there.' Like her hero Harry Potter there was a whole new personality waiting to be heard: a rebel in hiding.

Joanne continued to read voraciously, consuming an eclectic mix of James Bond and Jane Austen, who would remain her favourite author. She has read *Emma* some twenty times. When she was fourteen her great aunt gave her *Hons and Rebels*, the witty autobiography of Jessica Mitford. Joanne was bewitched, not just because it is an amusing and diverting read but because it was a true story of a real person. Jessica Mitford became the lifelong heroine of the impressionable teenager and, in no small measure, influenced her path to fulfilment: 'I found her inspiring because she was a brave and idealistic person – the qualities I most admire.'

The young Rowling also recognized a kindred spirit in the crusading Ms Mitford despite their very different back-grounds. Jessica was born in 1917, the sixth child of Lord Redesdale and, more significantly, one of the famous sisters who brightened the twentieth century in a notorious and brilliant manner. Nancy was the acclaimed writer of *The Pursuit of Love* and *Love in a Cold Climate*, Diana Mitford married the British fascist Sir Oswald Mosley and Unity, the most controversial, cavorted with the Nazis in Berlin and was a friend of Hitler. Jessica, a socialist and feminist, was the rebel – a characteristic that particularly attracted Joanne.

The very first paragraph of *Hons and Rebels* draws attention to the picturesque names of the historic villages of the Cotswolds where Jessica was born: Stow-on-the-Wold, Chipping Norton, Minster Lovell, Burford. Joanne Rowling loves fanciful names, which perhaps explains why she prefers to call Chipping Sodbury her place of birth rather than plain old Yate and why her own collection of names for the Harry Potter books owes much to a gazetteer. She is probably the most imaginative deviser of names for her characters since Dickens thought up Pecksniff, Quilp, Uriah Heep and a hundred more.

Mitford introduces her own village of Swinbrook with an observation that, in the tiny village post office, there were 'four kinds of sweets – toffee, acid drops, Edinburgh Rock and butterscotch – displayed in the same four large cut-glass jars ranged in the window'. Harry Potter finds fictional bliss in the sweet shop Honeydukes where he discovers a host of exotic sweets including Every Flavour Beans, Fizzing Whizzbees, peppermint creams shaped like toads and jars of Cockroach Cluster.

The Mitford girls had a wonderfully eccentric childhood where they made up names and games and terrorized a succession of governesses. Nowhere is that more pricelessly illustrated than when their mother introduced a contest with a prize of half a crown to the child who could offer the best budget for a young couple living on £500 ($750) a year: 'Nancy ruined the contest by starting her list of expenditures with "Flowers . . . £490".' The Mitford girls made up stories, dressed up in costumes and invented their own special language called Boudledidge. They thought up strange games and even stranger nicknames like Debo, Boud, Decca [Jessica] and Tuddemy who was their long-suffering only brother Tom.

All importantly Jessica Mitford could remember what it was like to be a child. She wrote: 'I envied the children of literature to whom interesting things were always happening. Oliver Twist was so lucky to live in a fascinating orphanage!' Not only did she read voraciously, like Joanne, she was also affected by what she read and would fantasize about herself as the heroine. She would be Jane Eyre, 'painfully thin and pale of face but steadfast of spirit'. She was the 'tall, serious, dark-eyed sixth-form prefect' of one of Angela Brazil's school stories.

Crucially when she was fourteen, the same age at which Joanna read *Hons and Rebels*, Decca was intensely moved by reading the anti-war novel *Cry Havoc* by Beverley Nichols which depicted the horrors of First World War bombing raids and urged total disarmament: 'I was enormously impressed with the originality and force of its arguments'. Jessica Mitford was constrained by Swinbrook just as Joanne Rowling's spirit was imprisoned in Tutshill. She 'glimpsed another world; a world of London bed-sitters, art students, writers . . . a world of new and different ideas . . . a world from which Swinbrook would seem as antiquated as a feudal stronghold'.

The Swinbrook of the late 1920s could have been the Tutshill of the late 1970s. Truly Joanne Rowling had found a kindred spirit. And Jessica Mitford's ultimate escape was utterly thrilling to the fourteen-year-old Joanne. She ran away or, more precisely, she eloped for a mixture of love and ideals to the Spanish Civil War. The object of her affection was Esmond Romilly, nephew of Winston Churchill, communist sympathizer and romantic demigod. Before they left they bought an expensive camera as war reporting equipment and charged it to Decca's father's account at the Army and Navy Stores. Joanne loved her new heroine's audacity and secretly wished she had the nerve to do something like that.

Ten years later Joanne too would make her way to a warmer climate when she moved to Portugal. But that is in the future. Perhaps she should have noted that the great romance ended sadly as a footnote in *Hons and Rebels*. Esmond Romilly died, killed in action in November 1941 at the age of twenty-three.

A sense of broadening horizons was contributing to Joanne flourishing at Wyedean School despite its obvious drawbacks. She still had to cope with a great malaise of education in Britain – namely bullying and the torment it causes those ill-equipped to deal with it. A schoolfriend recalls, 'Anyone who was intelligent or had ambition was at best ignored and usually bullied and picked on, even by teachers, as being swotty.' Joanne had to confront her own demons when a girl from her year attacked her in school. Never the biggest girl for her age and only 5ft 4ins fully grown, she fought back to the best of her ability. She later recalled, 'I didn't have a choice. It was hit back or lie down and play dead. For a few days I was quite famous because she hadn't managed to flatten me. The truth was, my locker was right behind me and it held me up.'

This particular incident failed to turn Joanne Rowling into a feared opponent at Wyedean and she spent a nervous few weeks avoiding her classroom thug. Suddenly popping over to the science block to get the lunch money from her mother seemed an attractive way of passing the morning break. Not surprisingly it reinforced her revulsion against bullying – in pupils, in teachers and, later, in lovers.

The vile Draco Malfoy and his two brutish henchmen Crabbe and Goyle personify the school bully in the Harry Potter series. Harry and, in particular, Ron Weasley are forever waging a battle against Slytherin's worst who, as yet, have no redeeming features whatsoever. Draco adheres to the finest psychological theory about bullies that they are cowards at heart. When faced with the prospect of encountering the unknown in the Forbidden Forest he reveals his true colours: 'The Forest?' he repeated, and he didn't sound quite as cool as usual. 'We can't go in there at night – there's all sorts of things in there – werewolves, I heard.' And later . . . 'Malfoy let out a terrible scream and bolted'.

One of Joanne's contemporaries at Wyedean was a small blond boy who may have been the inspiration for bullied, put-upon, runtish Neville Longbottom in the Harry Potter books. This particular boy is described by a friend of Joanne's as looking 'a lot younger than his age with a halo of blond hair and an angelic look like a choirboy. He was very shy and softly spoken and, as you can imagine, suffered as a result. He was bullied and had a horrible time.'

Bullying by teachers is an even greater anathema to Joanne Rowling, who believes it to be 'the shabbiest thing you can do'. Wyedean had its share and those ingredients were put into the melting pot of Snape's character. A schoolteacher can be stern and strict, even severe, without being a bully. Lucy Shepherd, Joanne's favourite teacher, was firm but never resorted to bullying a student. Joanne has always understood how, 'it's very easy to be a bully', particularly when she became a teacher herself.

Wyedean has recognized that bullying is a problem schools should confront. In a recent survey two of its female teachers admitted that they were bullied at school themselves. One of them observed, 'Bullies are sad because they aren't liked very much.' Pertinently, those who took part in the survey were all female, reinforcing the point that bullying is just as much a problem for girls as it is for boys, existing across the entire school system. And the fictional Hogwarts does not escape.

Hogwarts is an interesting creation because, as all the students are boarders, it is mistakenly thought to be a private school. John Nettleship is adamant that Hogwarts is broadly speaking a state comprehensive school. Certainly attendance seems to bear no relation to financial status, nor do pupils have to sit an entrance exam. The Weasley family, who have sent all their seven children there, barely have two 'sickles' to rub together. It is the ghastly Dudley Dursley who goes to a fee-paying private school, his father's alma mater Smeltings. Mr Nettleship explains, Joanne herself has pointed out that people read into these books exactly what they want to, which is why people who are in favour of boarding schools think it is all great. But Joanne herself is in favour of comprehensives and Hogwarts is a comprehensive school.'

Joanne never had any desire to go to boarding school, a point she has made repeatedly. She has also made it clear that her own daughter would never go to one. It is ironic, therefore, that the Harry Potter books have been suggested as a reason for an unexpected halt in the twenty-year decline of British boarding schools. In particular the number of girls boarding has increased and Nick Ward, chairman of the Boarding Schools Association, confirms that many parents have cited the Potter books as sparking an interest. It may also coincide with the fact that the average wage in Britain is on the increase and more people have money to spend on education.

Hogwarts is a boarding school primarily because J. K. Rowling would have enormous difficulty concocting a plot if it were not. The boarding school is a well-worn literary location in children's literature, so much so that one unkind, if witty, critic described the Harry Potter novels as 'Billy

Bunter on broomsticks'. Joanne recognizes the usefulness of Hogwarts being a boarding school. She admits in an interview with the on-line magazine, *Salon*, 'There is something liberating about being transported into the kind of surrogate family which boarding school represents, where the relationships are less intense and the boundaries perhaps more clearly defined.'

There was nothing particularly liberating for Joanne in woodwork and metalwork classes. She was hopeless. Like all good mothers Anne Rowling proudly kept a misshapen, ugly flat teaspoon which Joanne had made from endlessly hammering a lump of metal. It was no good for spooning sugar, but could be used for stirring or perhaps even as a screwdriver. A photograph frame consisting mainly of glue confirmed that Joanne was not a practical person. She even managed to break her arm playing the non-contact sport of netball. In a small way she was already following her heroine's example: Jessica Mitford had broken her arm twice by the age of ten.

CHAPTER FOUR

Goodbye to the Forest

'Home was a difficult place to be.'

IN THE 1998 FILM *Hilary and Jackie*, which features the tragic story of Jacqueline du Pré, there is a heartbreaking scene when the virtuoso cellist, played by Emily Watson, drops her bow during a recital. It marks a terrible moment when multiple sclerosis begins its march through her body. It is impossible to say when the first signs of MS, as it is widely known, hit Joanne's mother Anne – perhaps a test tube slipping through her fingers in a laboratory at school or a cup spilling tea on the carpet at Church Cottage.

Joanne remembers that she was twelve when her mother found difficulty in lifting a teapot. William Clark, who taught rural science and chemistry at Wyedean, became aware of a problem after Anne had a fall at school. Shirley Nettleship recalls her friend experiencing pins and needles in her hand when she was trying to play the guitar. When Anne was thirty-five and Joanne fifteen, doctors gave a proper diagnosis that it was multiple sclerosis and

the true horror of having to live with a progressively crippling disease struck the Rowling
household. One of the most poignant things Joanne
has ever said was on *Desert Island Discs.* Having
explained that her mother had a 'galloping' form of
the disease, she confessed, 'Home was a difficult
place to be.'

Anne Rowling was a woman full of fizz about
whom no one had a bad word to say. The cliché
about 'living life to the full' truly applied to the
raven-haired mother of two who never failed to put
her family's interest first and only stopped rushing
about to stick her nose in a book. She had an
infectious giggle that provoked much laughter in
those around her. John Nettleship recalls the
morning when he was walking up the path to the
science block at Wyedean with Anne and his
statuesque wife Shirley: 'As usual the milkman had
left two bottles of milk for the day. He'd left one of
the new short bottles and one of the old taller types.
"Look at those milk bottles," said Anne. "The
milkman's left an Anne and a Shirley." She just saw
them like that at once and I always thought it was a
lovely illustration of the sort of humour she would
put into everything. She was so vivacious.'

Anne's natural energy and the desire not to be a
sit-at-home housewife when her children were a
little older led her to her job at Wyedean. Her
husband Pete was moving steadily up the
executive ladder as a chartered engineer at Rolls-
Royce and she wanted to contribute more to the

household than the ironing. The job was ideal because it meant she still had plenty of daily contact with Joanne and Di. John Nettleship observes, 'She was a very child-centred person and ideal to have dealing with the pupils. The children would learn a lot from the technicians even though they weren't directly taught by them. Anne was totally supportive of the educational enterprise. She was a person of the highest standards.'

Joanne, despite her natural inclination towards privacy, revealed her feelings about her mother's illness to the *Scotland on Sunday* newspaper to highlight MS Awareness week in April 2001. The word 'awareness' is apt. The Rowlings, like thousands of other families affected by the disease, were unaware of it until its destructive presence was sharing their home. Eventually, when Anne was thirty-four, she was referred for hospital tests which revealed that 'she had a lack of protein in her spinal fluid'. Still no one put a name to her condition. It would be another year of pins and needles spreading over her body before she and Pete were told the awful truth that it was multiple sclerosis.

Joanne, in her affectionate and moving account of her mother and the illness that afflicted her, revealed the heartbreak of watching the disease get a grip: 'Some days she could lift the teapot, others she couldn't, but she was still zipping through the ironing like a demon and working as a laboratory technician at school, and still playing the guitar, for

God's sake, so obviously it wasn't anything very serious.'

MS is a disease of the central nervous system and a condition that remains largely a mystery to modern medicine. Mistakenly many people assume it is a muscular problem, or a wasting disease, simply because so little is known about it and because it invariably affects movement. In basic terms the information the brain sends down to the body's nerve ends becomes scrambled. That is why Anne Rowling could not pick up the teapot. Research has yet to find a cause or cure. One widely-held theory is that it is an infection triggered by one or more viruses, which may explain why its severity or progress varies considerably between sufferers.

By an unfortunate coincidence William Clark was diagnosed with the condition at the same time as Anne and shared the same consultant, Mr Langton Hewer at Frenchay Hospital in Bristol. Mr Clark recalls, 'Anne had a very virulent strain of the disease. One day she had a fall at school and left very abruptly.' He made a point of telling his students all about his illness and how it affected his life. As a sufferer of MS he could be considered lucky in that he has had the disease for twenty-six years and is still alive, although no longer teaching. Anne Rowling was not so fortunate.

Mr Clark remembers that she would have days when she was her normal, pleasant self and other off-days when 'she was not so good'. Shortly after proper diagnosis she had to give up her job. John Nettleship recalls, 'She was heartbroken when she was diagnosed with this illness because it meant she couldn't fulfil her role as a technician so easily. Anne would be washing test tubes and her fingers could no longer be relied on to hold them. The thought that she was failing in her duty in some way was much worse to her than the thought that she'd got a problem with the illness. She was not at all consumed with self-pity. Anne had enormous will-power and it was hard to believe she would ever succumb to this terrible illness.'

At home there were tears for Joanne and Di when the awful nature of their mother's 'galloping' disease became a reality. Church Cottage was littered with explanatory pamphlets and booklets about the disease – at least what little information was available. Typically Anne read everything she could lay her hands on to explain the illness. Some days she could walk only in a jerky motion and seemed to be deteriorating rapidly, but then there would be spells when she appeared almost back to normal. The bad days would gradually outnumber the good ones. 'The more the illness progressed, the more serious she became,' observes John Nettleship sadly. 'Her light-heartedness and spontaneity did tend to fade a bit.'

When she eventually gave up work, Anne had the problem of what to do with her days. Sylvia Lewis remembers that she used to go next door and clean the church – just for something to do – and the girls would often pop back and keep her company. It was a curious situation because the Rowlings were not churchgoers even though St Luke's was just over the garden fence. The two girls never attended Sunday school or services there but about once a year they would sign the church's visitors' book.

St Luke's is an unpretentious country church with wooden benches, a stone floor and a slightly musty smell, a small haven from the noise of cars speeding through the village or the children shrieking and shouting in the playground of Tutshill Primary School next door. The first signature of Joanne Rowling is on 2 June 1976, when she was ten. It is neat and legible and very similar to her grown-up author's signature. After her name she has carefully written 'Tutshill, Chepstow, Gwent', which is her correct postal address although the village itself is in Gloucestershire. Joanne signed again on 10 September 1977 and both sisters signed on 4 November 1977 when Joanne was twelve and Di ten. It must have been a very slow day at Church Cottage. After a gap Joanne signed the book twice more, on 22 April 1981 and lastly on 11 October 1981 when she was sixteen. Perhaps she had gone into the church to help her mother or perhaps she had decided to offer a prayer. Each entry is simple and serious.

As Hogwarts becomes a place of liberation for Harry Potter, so Wyedean took away some of the pressure Joanne was feeling because of the sad situation at home. Her chosen A-levels of English, French and German were allowing her to flourish intellectually – no more chemistry lessons meant no more potions. She was introduced to the theatre with a trip to Stratford-upon-Avon to see *King Lear*. Shakespeare often requires a level of attention that many pupils find difficult to muster, but Joanne loved it – the play and the experience. Up until the school trips she had been limited to pantomimes with her mother and father. After *King Lear* her class went to see *The Winter's Tale*, in which Hermione is the leading female character, and which would eventually give rise to Harry Potter's know-all friend, Hermione Granger. If a survey were conducted among schoolchildren to think of a famous literary Hermione they would be certain to name J. K. Rowling's creation rather than that of William Shakespeare.

A new boy called Séan Harris started at Wyedean in the upper sixth form. His father was in the army and had been posted to the base across from the school. He was a fresh face, a change from the old school gang of which Joanne had begun to tire. Joanne and Séan became instant and lasting friends. He was just that bit different, an outsider with a Spandau Ballet haircut. Joanne Rowling, lover of new wave music, supporter of Greenpeace and Amnesty International, warmed to him. 'He was the coolest man in school,' she recalled. And he had a car, a turquoise Ford Anglia that spelt escape from a situation that was becoming more and more oppressive for Joanne. It was blissful relief from an environment where the height of excitement was a smoke outside the chip shop at lunchtimes. Séan and Jo would take to the open road, the M4 motorway, and trundle over to Bristol and Bath or in the other direction to Newport and Cardiff to bars and discos, clubs and concerts. Or they would park underneath the Severn Bridge and gaze out over the estuary, making grand plans to make a difference. Suddenly the world was a bigger place.

Joanne paid Séan the compliment of dedicating the second Harry Potter book to him with the inscription: 'getaway driver and foul weather friend'. She also paid tribute to that first vehicle of freedom by making the Weasley family car a turquoise Ford Anglia. This magic flying car becomes a symbol of rescue throughout the book. First it is the Weasley brothers' mode of transport when they come to rescue Harry from his virtual prison at number four Privet Drive, where his uncle has locked him in his bedroom: 'Ron was leaning out of the back window of an old turquoise car, which was parked in mid-air.' Secondly it transports Harry and Ron to Hogwarts after they miss the school express: 'Harry could feel the seat vibrating beneath him, hear the engine, feel his hands on his knees and his glasses on his nose.' Thirdly, and perhaps most importantly, it rescues them from the giant spiders in the Forbidden Forest where it has become a wild car: 'Harry gave the car a grateful pat as it reversed back into the Forest and disappeared from view.' Joanne was very fond of Séan's beaten-up old car and was happy to let the illustrator Cliff Wright paint it for the front cover of the children's edition of *The Chamber of Secrets*.

On 23 April 1983 Anne Rowling made her will. George Francis, a solicitor and friend who lived nearby in Tutshill, prepared the document for her. She was just thirty-eight but knew it was the sensible thing to do, especially as she was unlikely to be able to work much longer. She left everything to Pete but if he did not survive her she split her estate; one half to her sister Marian and husband Leslie and the other to the Multiple Sclerosis Society. She would have wholeheartedly applauded Joanne's involvement with the MS Society Scotland, and doubtless would have been out rattling a collecting tin if she had still been alive.

In her final year Joanne became head girl, a position voted for partly by staff and partly by the pupils. It was testimony to her popularity and maturity. Her mother's illness and the cloud over Church Cottage had somehow launched a sunnier, more sociable Joanne on the world. Her work was also showing such promise that it was decided she would seek a place at Oxford University to read modern languages. Anne and Pete, who had not been to university, were thrilled at the prospect. John Nettleship believes it was the Rowlings' ambition that their daughters should see their education through and not have the struggle they themselves had as a young couple in their early twenties. Clearly both parents had an intelligence and talent that could easily have absorbed a university education. 'Pete was a pretty clever bloke and it was one of their frustrations that they didn't go on to university and went through life the hard way. He had to qualify through putting the time into going to night school. They were a pair of very talented people.'

Joanne sat an entrance test for Oxford and was put on a reserve list awaiting the results of her A-levels. Eventually she was rejected. Mr Nettleship is adamant that she failed to get in because she went to a comprehensive school. It is his opinion that she was discriminated against because of her school in a way that mirrors the story of schoolgirl Laura Spence. Widely reported on the front pages of the British press in 2000, it was claimed that Laura was turned down by Oxford University because she attended a state school, rather than a private school. Her fate provoked an outburst from Chancellor Gordon Brown about the elitism of Oxford and Cambridge. He blasted the old boy network and the old school tie: 'I say it is time to end the Old Britain where what matters are the privileges you were born into, not the potential you actually have. I say it is time these old universities open their doors to women and to people from all backgrounds.'

Mr Nettleship remembers Joanne was on a reserve list along with another girl who had been at

Wyedean but whose parents sent her to an independent sixth-form college to sit her A-levels. Joanne achieved two A-grades (English and French) and one B-grade (German) while her former classmate had managed just one A and two Bs in the same subjects. And yet it was the other girl who was successful. 'I believe she was favoured because of where her parents had been able to afford to send her. It gave her an unfair advantage. We were all following the situation very keenly because we would get a blow-by-blow account of it every morning from her mum when she came into work. It did seem very unfair at the time.

'We wouldn't have had many pupils at Wyedean considered Oxbridge material – perhaps two or three serious contenders a year – and normally none of them would succeed.'

A close friend at Wyedean recalls, 'You would face enormous hurdles coming from Wyedean and, at the time we were there, Oxbridge was perceived as being impossible for comprehensive people to get into.' Joanne has never spoken out in public about it but in retrospect it is rather gratifying that Oxford missed out on J. K. Rowling. As John Nettleship suggests, 'If she had gone there, she might never have got round to writing these precious books.'

Despite that rejection Joanne remained keen to move on with her life. She has never looked to the past.

On Saturday 28 April 2001 the class of '83 at Wyedean held a reunion at the school which was one of those jolly affairs at which the boys and girls of the previous generation appraise how they have respectively aged. They were all in their mid-thirties, of course, and the boy who had caught the eye of the teenage Joanne was there. Alas, his former admirer was not. Her contemporaries would have loved to see her, perhaps to bask in the reflected glory of her achievements, but the harsh truth is that Joanne had no desire to renew their acquaintance. Paula Whitehouse, the headmaster's secretary, admits that the school has twice asked her to go back and see them but, as yet, with no favourable response from its most famous pupil.

Joanne's main goal as an intelligent, free-thinking eighteen-year-old was to get out of Wyedean and away from the Forest of Dean. But there is some cause for pride at the school. Her experiences there run through the Harry Potter stories like rivulets. The friends she made like Séan Harris, the teachers who taught her – John Nettleship and Lucy Shepherd, for instance – and the classrooms in which she spent her time all influenced her. As John Nettleship says, 'Joanne was a shrewd observer. I think that by the time she had been there for seven years she would have built up a great store of knowledge from what she had overheard and seen.'

Joanne has said she can remember clearly what it was like each year of her childhood and adolescence. At Wyedean she did the growing up that Harry, Hermione and Ron are doing at Hogwarts in the Potter chronicles. Wyedean's importance, therefore, is not to be taken lightly, although the school and its surroundings will always remind Joanne painfully of her mother, Anne.

And then there is the great and magical Forest of Dean which, for all Joanne's wish to leave it behind, fired her imagination with its myths and legends, not to mention the spectacular scenery. Phyl Lewis, who taught ceramics and sculpture at Wyedean and who runs a studio in the heart of the Forest in the village of Bream declares, 'You couldn't live by the Forest or the Wye Valley and not be inspired by its history and traditions. When I was a child I'd be in the Forest until dusk. If you saw a fairy ring of mushrooms you were awe-inspired. A few yards further on and you would be overcome by a feeling of evil lurking there.'

Tales of witchcraft and curses abound in local lore. As recently as 1906 a woman from Cinderford called Ellen Hayward faced charges that she 'unlawfully did use a certain craft or means or device to wit by pretended witchcraft deceive and impose on one of His Majesty's Subjects'. The woman, known as Old Ellen, described herself as a herbalist and dresser of sores, cuts and wounds.

In the first year at Hogwarts the students studied Herbology three times a week with 'a dumpy little witch called Professor Sprout'. The lessons took place in the greenhouses behind the castle, where they learnt how to nurture many strange and unusual plants and fungi and were taught their uses in different spells. It is Professor Sprout who, crucially, in *Harry Potter and the Chamber of Secrets*, cultivates the mandrake plants which will restore the petrified victims of the Basilisk, the terrifying serpent guarding the chamber.

In 1892 a lead tablet was discovered in the village of Dymock on the north edge of the Forest of Dean. The tablet contained a curse placed upon a woman called Sarah Ellis, whose name was written backwards at the top of the tablet. 'The Dymock Curse' invoked the name of eight spirits 'to make this person banish away from the place and country. Amen to my desire Amen.' [In *Harry Potter and the Philosopher's Stone* we are introduced to the Mirror of Erised, which is 'desire' spelt backwards.] Knowledge of the curse allegedly drove Sarah insane and she eventually killed herself. The custom of the time for dealing with suicide victims led to Sarah being buried at a crossroads with a stake through her body.

One of the great legends of the Forest is the tale of one young man's efforts to see the daughter of a local man who was fiercely protective of her. One summer afternoon the old man was seated in his garden when he saw the unwelcome young suitor pass by. Having made sure he had gone on his way, the old man fell asleep in the afternoon sun while his daughter prepared their dinner inside the house. Later he awoke to see a hare staring at the house. Quickly, he fetched his gun and fired a shot at the animal, which he thought would make a tasty meal. Unfortunately he only succeeded in wounding the hare in one of its hind legs as it bolted off. A short time later the young man emerged from the field into which the hare had run. He was limping.

It is an early example of what J. K. Rowling calls an Animagus, a wizard or witch who can turn him or herself into an animal. At the very beginning of *Harry Potter and the Philosopher's Stone* Mr Dursley is astounded to see what he thinks is a large tabby cat reading a map. His eyes are not playing tricks on him, however, as the cat is in fact Professor McGonagall.

The Forest of Dean is indeed 'a little country on its own' and growing up there inevitably had an effect on Joanne and on J. K. Rowling the author. She may well have been more affected by the books she read and undoubtedly her family life was more important but the Forest had a considerable influence on her, which should not be underestimated. If nothing else, as she has admitted, Hagrid, the giant Hogwarts gamekeeper, speaks in a West Country accent.

CHAPTER FIVE

Natural Woman

'She was an internalized person who was not in an active relationship with the outside world.'

THE UNIVERSITY OF EXETER was an odd choice for a student who entertained thoughts of mixing with freethinking radicals who would change the world. It had the dubious distinction of being featured in *The Official Sloane Ranger Handbook,* a satirical look at young upper middle-class girls in the early eighties in Britain. 'Sloane Ranger' was coined from the old Western hero The Lone Ranger and Sloane Square in Chelsea. Sloane Rangers were objects of gentle fun. If Joanne had looked in the *Handbook* she would have discovered that the places to drink for students (G & Ts of course) were the Cowley Bridge Inn, Double Locks pub, the Passage at Topsham and Crediton Wine Bar. As for parties, 'two and a half hours away by 125 to Paddington – and you do your shopping in London'. At Exeter the former public school students were known as 'Welly' and the rest, which would include Joanne, were 'non-Welly'. Unsurprisingly the university boasted one of the highest ratios of cars per student in the country. Joanne, however, could not drive.

She had not taken a 'gap year' after leaving Wyedean, so was plunged straight into student life on campus. It was not at all what she expected. She also had to contend with the big fish/small fish syndrome. At Wyedean she had been head girl. At Exeter she was a nervous undergraduate, just turned eighteen, from a provincial state school. One of her tutors Ray Davison recalls, 'She had a problem settling down here.'

Exeter had been a relatively safe choice and Joanne had been guided to a large extent by her parents. It was a step away from home but not a huge one – a two-hour drive from Church Cottage and even quicker by train from Chepstow, changing at Bristol Temple Meads. From Exeter St David's station the university is a mile's walk away, mainly uphill, to a campus which is an invigorating place full of lawns, mature trees, tennis courts and birdsong. On one of the lawns is a Barbara Hepworth statue entitled *Mother and Child*.

The university was granted its charter in December 1955 and was therefore established well before that title was afforded every polytechnic in the land. When Joanne was looking at choices after her Oxford disappointment, Exeter was the only university south-west of Bristol, which itself boasted an excellent reputation but was a little too close to home. The campus has a breathtaking position on a hill over-looking the ancient cathedral city and county town of Devon. Yvette Cowles, a fellow undergraduate, recalls ringing her mother and telling her, 'It's so beautiful here. It's just lovely.'

The quiet peace of academia did not stretch to the halls of residence, which were Joanne's first home after leaving Church Cottage. She was in Jessie Montgomery Hall, a red-brick slab of a building where the students have soulless little rooms. It is more likely to have inspired the television series *Prisoner Cell Block H* than Hogwarts School of Witchcraft and Wizardry. Joanne made it as homely as possible with her books, her sketchpads and her acoustic guitar, but it was never going to match her room at home. To get to the teaching blocks and, more importantly, the students' guild coffee shop and bars involved struggling up a steep path known by one and all as Cardiac Hill for obvious reasons.

At least there were things to do in the evening in Exeter. The Odeon Film Centre was showing three films the week Joanne arrived: *Educating Rita*, *Octopussy* and *Porky's II*. And the Northcott Theatre, within the boundaries of the campus, is one of the leading provincial companies in the country. The Tom Stoppard farce *Dirty Linen* was the main attraction during her first term.

Joanne's major problem at first was finding students with whom she had anything in common. The best place to do this was in the students' guild building on campus, called Devonshire House. The focal point was the Devonshire House coffee bar: 'Much more than just coffee . . . Pies, Pasties, Meat or Vegetable kebabs, Toasted sandwiches.' It became a home from home for Joanne and, when she received an honorary degree from Exeter in 1999, one of her old university friends suggested it would have been more appropriate to put an engraved ashtray in the Devonshire House coffee bar.

Something strange happened to Joanne at university. The Hermione-like school swot influence so pronounced at the beginning of her teens, had practically evaporated at the end of them. The girl who wore National Health spectacles had become a flamboyant, voluptuous young woman with contact lenses and perhaps more interest in a social life than an academic one. Yvette Cowles recalls, 'She wore long skirts and used to have this blue denim jacket she liked to wear. Jo was very shapely and she had this big hair, kind of back-combed and lacquered, and lots of heavy eyeliner. I think she was quite popular with the guys.'

Two factors influenced the change in Joanne. First it was her new-found freedom away from home. Yvette observes that she would never have guessed that her friend came from such a provincial backwater. Second she did not particularly shine in her chosen degree course, so the enthusiasm to study was not as strong as it might have been if she had been taking an English major. One of her tutors, Martin Sorrell, says, 'She was a straight middle-of-the-road student who was not in any way out of place but clearly wasn't ambitious in this area of languages.' Professor Keith Cameron, who taught her throughout her degree course and was appointed head of Modern Languages during Joanne's last year there in 1987, concurs, 'She was not as gifted in languages as some.'

Joanne ended up studying French; a decision influenced by her parents, who thought it might lead more easily to a job than a nebulous English degree. A language degree was evidence of a skill which would be useful pursuing work as a bi-lingual secretary or translator. Perhaps her always practical father, who had become a chartered engineer without the benefit of a university education, had voiced doubts over the merits of pursuing an English degree. Joanne told Angela Levin of the *Daily Mail*, 'I wanted to do English but felt everyone would say: "What's the use of that?" Although I longed to be a writer, I never thought it would be possible, so told only close friends.'

So Joanne was stuck with studying French and Classics. At least the teachers were interesting. The author Brian Clapp in his history of the University of Exeter writes: 'Mild eccentricity has always been an agreeable part of the academic scene. There was a degree of formality in the modern languages department. Yvette Cowles explains, 'You didn't call them "Martin" or "Ray". It would always be "Mr" or "Professor". I think it was partly because it was quite a traditional place and also the style of the course itself. It was very literature-based. It didn't really equip you for life in France. When everyone had to go and spend a year in France, I found I could talk about the philosophy of the country but I couldn't tell you how to boil a kettle.

'Jo liked the Classics side of things. She liked those mythological stories. That interested her. I suppose that's not a surprise.'

The 'shrewd observer' remembered by John Nettleship would have enjoyed the company of the modern languages faculty and they, in return, were intrigued by a girl whom Ray Davison remembers as 'very dreamy'. He adds, 'She was an internalized person who was not in an active relationship with the outside world.'

She was certainly shrewd enough to know others saw her as a daydreamer. One particular lecturer was very patient and Joanne later recalled, 'His tolerance towards my frightening ignorance of his subject was awe-inspiring. The closest he ever came to admonishing me for my erratic attendance and propensity to lose every handout he gave me the moment we parted company was when he described me as sleepwalking around the place. This was said with an expression of mingled patience and amusement. I lived to regret repeating his remark to friends. It was sufficiently apt for them to repeat it more often than I found funny.'

Erratic attendance and losing work were not characteristics of which Hermione Granger would approve. The interesting point is that the 'new'

Joanne Rowling was enjoying herself. In many ways she had become a typical student. It is a testament to the regard in which she holds her university that she was happy to tell that story against herself for *Pegasus,* the house magazine of the Classics department after one lecturer, David Harvey, had written to her.

For her second year at Exeter Joanne moved into another block on campus called Lafrowda which was full of self-catering apartments, rather like a ski lodge. The rooms were no better than at Jessie Montgomery. They were small cubicles with single beds, basic university fare. She would have preferred to have been in Thomas Hall, a mansion house on the edge of the campus exclusively for women and with an identity and dormitory-like atmosphere all its own. A lawn dotted with large conifers sweeps down to the pale yellow house with its impressive brass front door. It is easy to imagine Harry Potter in his invisibility cloak darting down the grassy hill and hiding beneath the giant branches of a gnarled old fir before gingerly crossing the stream and sprinting for the door and the safety of the large common room complete with desks, wooden chairs and an old piano.

It was 1984 and Joanne had discovered The Smiths who were her favourite band then and now. One of her selections for *Desert Island Discs* was the classic 'Bigmouth Strikes Again', a minor chart hit in May 1986. She told Sue Lawley, 'I just love them for the guitar and for the lyrics which are so witty.'

The Smiths, with the inimitable Morrissey on vocals and the innovative Johnny Marr on lead guitar, were the darlings of both the critics and discerning students who eschewed Spandau Ballet, Culture Club and the New Romantics. Joanne would sit in her room trying to master Johnny Marr's chords to classics like 'What Difference Does It Make?' and 'Heaven Knows I'm Miserable Now'. 'I can see why she liked The Smiths,' observes Yvette Cowles. 'They were sort of melancholy and morose. I think that while Jo appeared quite tough and confident and a laugh and quite gregarious, she was actually pretty shy. In that respect she was a solitary person because she spent a lot of time living in her imagination. She was very much her own person.'

Joanne, just as she did among friends at Wyedean, displayed her talent for storytelling. Although she had a few boyfriends she always enjoyed the company of her female friends, an informal gang or sisterhood who discussed each other's problems, which were usually the men in their lives. Yvette recalls the stories well: 'She would write them using us as the characters. They were usually spy stories and we were all Mata-Hari type characters whom she would weave into the plot. I was a *femme fatale* called Snake Hips. But then we were all *femmes fatales* in the stories because we were all obviously so wonderful. And we always came out the winners.'

On fine summer evenings the girls would pile

into Katrina McKinnon's car and go to the Double Locks pub by the Exeter Canal. To reach the pub cars negotiate a narrow track for three-quarters of a mile, a route that becomes a good deal narrower and more hair-raising on the way home after closing time. It is a rabbit warren of a pub with low ceilings, rickety wooden benches and oak tables around which a dozen students could squeeze – rather like The Three Broomsticks in Hogsmeade. Three nights a week there was live music, usually jazz. In summer the girls would fill the benches by the water's edge and stagger in and out laden with trays of beer, most of which would be spilt on the journey. Joanne, like a true Bond fan, rarely drank beer, always preferring shorts, usually vodka.

The pub she most frequented is The Black Horse in the city centre. Joanne spent almost as much time in there as she did drinking coffee in the Devonshire House coffee bar. Yvette Cowles remembers one particular evening when the gang of some half-dozen girls, including Joanne, were making their way back from the pub to campus when they began a drunken rendition of 'You Make Me Feel Like A Natural Woman' by Aretha Franklin, followed by an equally boisterous version of the soul diva's 'Respect'. The good folk of Exeter were doubtless delighted by the noise.

A typical week for a student would comprise seven or eight hours of lectures and seminars and another four or five in tutorial. Beyond that students took responsibility for their own study.

Joanne did the minimum. Exams, however, reared their ugly head at the end of the second year and Joanne did not display any of Hermione's characteristics in her approach. For a start she forgot to register properly for her exam and was sent for by Ray Davison for a stern word. Joanne scraped through but it was decided it would suit her better if she dropped Greek and Roman Studies for her final two years. Time may show whether Hermione Granger's furious work ethic starts to falter as she grows older and she realizes there is more to life than exams and merit points.

The most pressing decision for Joanne at this stage was where to spend her year in France which was an essential part of the degree course. There were three options: to teach English part-time in a French school which was a scheme organized by the British Institute in Paris; to become a student at a French college; or to work for a French company. Joanne chose the first option and ended up living in Paris for her next academic year. It was the first time she tried teaching for herself.

Professor Cameron explains, 'The year in France is an opportunity to learn about French culture. The students build on their knowledge of language and fluency, both spoken and written. It gives them a greater maturity. More importantly in Joanne's case it gave her a better awareness of her own language and idiom. It provides a greater love of your own language. I have never met anyone who, as a result of this year, disliked the French.'

Joanne says she loved her time in Paris. She shared a flat with an Italian man called Fernando, a Spanish girl and a Russian woman. The Spanish girl was so obsessively tidy that Joanne, who was decidedly not, spent most of her time in her room reading so that she could avoid the kitchen. She told the Radio 4 literary programme *With Great Pleasure* that one Sunday she stayed in her room all day reading *A Tale of Two Cities* by Charles Dickens: 'When I emerged in the evening I walked straight into Fernando who looked absolutely horrified. I had mascara down my face and he assumed I had just received news of a death which I had – Sydney Carton's.' The unhappy Carton had taken the place of Charles Darnay at the guillotine because of his love for Darnay's wife Lucie and by his ultimate sacrifice finds salvation: 'It is a far, far better thing that I do than I have ever done; it is a far, far better rest that I go to than I have ever known.'

Joanne considers this 'the most perfect last line of a book ever written' and one that 'invariably makes her cry'. She has already written the last line of the Harry Potter series although readers will have to wait until the publication of Book Seven in a few years' time. It will be fascinating to learn the final fate of Voldemort, whose name translates from the French as 'Flight of Death'.

Joanne returned to Lafrowda for her final year. Many of her contemporaries had been doing a three-year degree course, so had graduated and moved on. That brought her and her fellow French students, a year older than most undergraduates, closer together, particularly in the evenings. Yvette recalls, 'We would all meet in the bar and afterwards go back to somebody's room for a drink and to sit chatting. Jo liked a drink. She liked to party and have a good time. But she did have a serious side and I wonder if this thing of being the life and soul was a cover. Outwardly you would never have guessed that there was any situation with her mother. I think she hid her vulnerabilities as part of a control thing. I always thought she was quite like the character of Rizzo in *Grease*, the dark-haired character who was a bit of a bad girl but was really quite soft. I always quite admired her.'

Joanne remained 'one of the girls' even though she had found her first serious boyfriend and began a relationship that would last on and off for several years. He was a fellow student, tall, dark and liked to go out drinking – a bit of a laddish type in a middle-class sort of way. Yvette observes, 'He was a typical student; she had the stronger personality. I always thought he was a bit wet. I seem to remember them being on the verge of splitting up at Exeter.'

During her last year, in March 1987, Joanne volunteered to help with the annual French play directed by Martin Sorrell. The play was a zany philosophical fantasy called *The Agricultural Cosmonaut* by the French dramatist Obaldia. Joanne was appointed wardrobe mistress. Professor Sorrell explains, 'I would describe it as a good, lively, fun spectacle. It was a good play for students because it's not too long and there are only three characters – a child of four, who was played by a student called Clare Woodcock, and her parents. The child is the cosmonaut of the title and goes missing. Her parents then indulge in a series of philosophical discussions. It's a bit mad.'

Joanne took her responsibilities seriously and went to all the rehearsals. Professor Sorrell recalls, 'She was a key member of the team because the costumes had to be just right. Her biggest concern was devising a costume for Clare, the cosmonaut. We improvised something quite brilliant, a sort of silvery all-in-one suit with a white helmet and breathing apparatus. I was impressed that she took part in the play because it's so easy just not to bother when you are a student. People sign up and then they are unreliable. But in this case the play went well and the costumes were great.'

The play ran for three nights at St Luke's Theatre, which although a university building is in a different part of Exeter. It was a sell-out which was quite surprising considering it was performed entirely in French.

The other principal preoccupation for Joanne at this time was her dissertation, a 3,000-word essay in French which counted towards her final degree. Professor Sorrell says, 'It tests your organizational skills.' His colleague Professor Cameron adds, 'There were signs that Joanne worked better in subjects which required a greater personal involvement from her, which is why her dissertation was her best piece of work.'

During her last year the prospect of 'finals' loomed ominously. Joanne did not approach them as Hermione Granger would have done. Yvette Cowles recalls, 'I don't remember Jo as being a desperately academic student. She always liked books and was obviously well-read but that gave her a different take on things, not an overtly academic one.'

Joanne spent a lot of time in the library. She had plenty of titles to choose from. The university has a million books, with something like 600,000 on the main campus alone. Joanne's interest was mainly in English and not her chosen subject of French. She was exceedingly bad at returning books she had borrowed and ran up a fine of £50 ($75) for overdue books, a considerable amount for a student.

One of the books she did read during her university days was *The Lord of the Rings*, the famous fantasy novel by the Oxford professor J. R. R. Tolkien. Joanne became a great admirer of the saga and her 1,000-page volume containing the entire story became battered and worn over the years. Aficionados love to draw comparisons between the Harry Potter books and the Tolkien epic. Both have a broadly similar strategy – exploring the eternal conflict between good and evil in relatively simple or black and white form. Tolkien was a cerebral academic, a philologist (studier of language) and a professor of medieval literature. His achievement, which Joanne herself has acknowledged, was to create a totally original mythology. His names for characters, beasts and objects are exotic and wonderful and, like Joanne's, roll off the tongue: Aragorn, Butterbur, Mugwort, Wormtongue and Bilbo Baggins contrast strikingly with some from the Potter stories like Aragog, Butterbeer, Muggles, Wormtail and Dudley Dursley. Both heroes, Harry and Frodo, his Tolkien counterpart, are naive orphans with unpleasant relatives: Harry has the Dursleys and Frodo the Sackville-Bagginses.

Both Tolkien and Rowling employ a friendly mentor or father-figure who allows the hero to grow but is ready to step in and rescue if necessary. Harry has Dumbledore, Frodo has Gandalf. The enemy in both cases is a 'Dark Lord', Sauron in *The Lord of the Rings* and Voldemort in the Harry Potter stories. In both series the Dark Lord has been crippled and is coming back to power slowly. Both are defeated not by might but by the hero being strong and good. Frodo is ultimately successful by not giving in to taking the power of the ring for himself. In the same way Harry beats Voldemort in *The Philosopher's Stone* by imagining himself giving the stone to Dumbledore, not by picturing himself assuming the power.

Wormtongue has strong parallels with Wormtail. Wormtongue is ensconced at the right hand of the King of Rohan, near enough to influence and spy on proceedings. Wormtail – also known as Peter Pettigrew – assumes the form of a rat and joins the Weasley family as a pet to keep informed of important events in the wizarding world. Both Wormtongue and Wormtail reveal their true colours as close but ultimately weak acolytes of the Dark Lord.

A crossover of ideas between two stories dealing with broadly similar themes involving magic and myth is not surprising. Two are particularly striking. *The Lord of the Rings* has the black, hooded Ringwraiths while *The Prisoner of Azkaban* introduces the black, hooded Dementors. Both have an extraordinary effect on the hero: 'Harry felt his own breath catch in his chest. The cold went deeper than his skin. It was inside his chest, it was inside his very heart . . .' and in Tolkien's work, 'the old wound throbbed with pain and a great chill spread towards Frodo's heart.'

Again in *Harry Potter and the Philosopher's Stone* Harry discovers The Mirror of Erised which, Dumbledore tells him, 'shows us nothing more or less than the deepest, most desperate desire of our hearts'. In Book Two of *The Fellowship of the Ring* Frodo comes across the Mirror of Galadriel. The Elf-lady tells him, 'Many things I can command the Mirror to reveal and to some I can show what they desire to see.'

Joanne Rowling has said *The Little White Horse* is the book that most influenced Harry Potter. Like all great authors she can assimilate ideas, whether they be from Tolkien, Jane Austen or Elizabeth Goudge, and use them to fertilize her own imagination. Asked if Tolkien's work influenced the Harry Potter series she replied, 'I think, if you set aside the fact that the books overlap in terms of dragons and wands and wizards, the Harry Potter books are very different, especially in tone. Tolkien created a whole mythology. I don't think anyone could claim that I have done that. On the other hand he didn't have Dudley.'

The creation of Harry Potter was still more than five years away when Joanne first read *The Lord of the Rings.* Clearly it had a substantial influence on her, as did other books from her childhood. Tolkien certainly lacks Rowling's wit as the Harry Potter series is very funny. It is hard to imagine Tolkien writing the scene in *The Prisoner of Azkaban* involving the book seller: 'It's been bedlam. I thought we'd seen the worst when we bought two hundred copies of The Invisible Book of Invisibility – cost a fortune and we never found them.'

Joanne had a happy time at Exeter and allusions to the county of Devon and her university life are dotted all over the Harry Potter stories. In *The Philosopher's Stone* the discoverer of the Elixir of Life, Nicolas Flamel, lives in Devon where he has reached the grand age of 665. Madam Z Nettles of Topsham seeks advice from an agony column about her fortune telling. The Weasley family live in a ramshackle house in Ottery St Catchpole. And then there is Professor Binns who features occasionally in the books and who, Joanne has admitted, was based entirely on a lecturer in the

Classics department at the university. Professor Binns is a teacher who fell asleep in front of the staff-room fire and died, and next morning got up to teach, leaving his body behind. His ghost continues to take the History of Magic class which is 'easily the most boring lesson' at Hogwarts: 'Professor Binns opened his notes and began to read in a flat drone like an old vacuum cleaner until everyone in the class was in a deep stupor . . .'

Joanne passed her finals and attained a 2:2, no more than an average degree for a student of her ability. She may have been inspired to do better if she had studied English, but her tutor Martin Sorrell says, 'I have no great sense of whether her degree did her any great favour or disfavour. From the point of view of personal ambition I am not totally for a writer doing an English degree.'

Graduation was a jolly, bright, sunny event in 1987. Everyone had dressed up, with the Sloane Ranger types in little black cocktail dresses and boys with Duran Duran haircuts looking incongruous in suits. Pete and Anne – in a wheelchair – were there to applaud their daughter. It was a proud day for them and when her name was called out Joanne, self-conscious in mortar board and gown, made her way on to the stage to be presented with her degree by Sir Rex Richards, the Chancellor of the University.

One of the honorary degrees of Doctor of Letters that day was presented to Glenda Jackson, who told the students that she prized the honour more than any of her acting awards. Her story was one to inspire those who set out from less than privileged beginnings. She had left school at sixteen and began her working life as a shop assistant in a Boots store. At the time of her degree the actress was filming for Ken Russell but it would not be long before she gave up that career for a new and successful one in politics, becoming an MP in 1992.

Joanne was destined to follow in Miss Jackson's footsteps as an honorary graduate of the University of Exeter. As Martin Sorrell observes, 'Quite clearly Joanne was waiting for her time to come.'

That time was still some way off.

Anne Rowling's condition had worsened considerably. She needed a wheelchair outside the house and by the time Joanne left university she needed a walking frame to get about her own home. The Tutshill butcher Geoff Roser used to drop off anything she needed at Church Cottage and remembers that without fail she would ask him, 'Now, are you sure it's not too much trouble?' Anne had become a popular figure in the village and there was widespread sympathy for her.

Joanne had been going through a period of drift in her life. She had taken a secretarial course for students who could speak more than one language – in her case English and French – but she was by her own admission a 'nightmare' as a secretary. After leaving Exeter she moved into a flat in Clapham, south-west London, with some girls from university and made ends meet with temping work, not knowing where she would be sent from one week to the next. One job was with a publisher where her duties included sending out rejection slips. At least during this period she learned to type at great speed, which was an invaluable skill for a budding writer.

Joanne was to a great extent appeasing the worries of her parents about her future. They were practical people and Anne naturally fretted that she would not be around to help in the years ahead. Joanne spent some time in London working for Amnesty International. She was excited at first but soon the lack of active involvement disappointed her aspirations. Yvette Cowles recalls, 'Jo was quite idealistic and I remember her being quite disillusioned. I don't think she was very happy there.' She worked in the African department, helping with research into human rights abuse in French-speaking countries, but never really fitted in. When her workmates went off to the pub for lunch Joanne would make an excuse and head off in the opposite direction to find a quiet place to write the adult novel she had begun. At one stage her excuses became so ridiculous that a colleague asked if she was having a lunchtime affair. Neither of the two adult novels she had written by the age of twenty-five has seen the light of day but she did get the habit of scribbling notes and paragraphs in cafés and bars, something which was to stand her in good stead when writing Harry Potter.

Joanne had another way of securing her privacy while working. Her parents had never had a taste for classical music and did not own a single piece of 'serious' music but Joanne had developed quite a taste for it. She was entirely self-taught, finding out what she liked by trial and error from buying lots of different cassette tapes. One of her favourites was Beethoven's *Appassionata* piano sonata which she used to play when temping as an audio typist. 'It used to stop people talking to me. I would put in my earplugs and pretend to be typing.'

Her boyfriend from Exeter had moved to Manchester and Joanne decided to join him there. It was not the happiest decision she ever made, the beginning of what she has called a year of misery, but it led to the momentous flash of inspiration that changed her life. 'Given the chance,' she reveals, 'I would not go back and warn myself against moving to Manchester or taking the office job or starting that very bad novel.'

Joanne was in a far from buoyant mood when she sat gazing at the same stretch of English countryside for forty minutes on a train back to London after a weekend of fruitless flat-hunting in Manchester. She could have thought of many things: whether she was right to leave London, how her mother was doing back in Church Cottage, how her father was coping. She could have thought of the Black Horse or the Devonshire House coffee bar and more carefree times. She thought of none of these, however, because Joanne Rowling has always been a dreamer and, as she gazed out of the carriage window at some equally forlorn-looking black and white Friesian cows, she thought of a train transporting a boy to a boarding school for wizards: 'All of a sudden the idea for Harry just appeared in my mind's eye. I can't tell you why or what triggered it. But I saw the idea of Harry and the wizard school very plainly. I suddenly had this basic idea of a boy who didn't know who he was, who didn't know he was a wizard until he got his invitation to wizard school. I have never been so excited by an idea.'

Unusually, to her frustration, Joanne had neither pen nor paper with her that June evening so she closed her eyes to see everything inside her own head. She thought about the main character Harry, although she had not set upon his name then. She pictured him as a scrawny little boy. She concentrated on the school and the people Harry might meet there. She told Lindsey Fraser that by the end of the journey she had thought of Ron Weasley, based on Séan Harris, Hagrid the gamekeeper, the character she has said she would most like to meet in real life, and the school ghosts Nearly Headless Nick and Peeves. At this early stage she did not have names for all her characters. They would come later using, among other sources, gazetteers and *Brewer's Dictionary of Phrase and Fable*.

Most of all Joanne considered the school itself and what it might be like. She imagined a Scottish setting because Scotland had been important to her parents and parts of it were wild and windy. She thought of a castle but not one in particular she had seen. Hogwarts is a combination of many buildings: Tintern Abbey near Chepstow perhaps, Thomas Hall at Exeter University or a peculiar construction erected for a school project in the main hall at Wyedean when she was thirteen. They all went into the melting pot that became Hogwarts. Later, back in her room, she frantically jotted down what she could remember from the train in a small, cheap, flimsy notebook – the very first Harry Potter document.

To suggest that Harry Potter instantly became an all-consuming passion for Joanne is an exaggeration. At this early stage, June 1990, publication was seven years away. It was, however, a welcome diversion from the tedium of a life that seemed to be going nowhere. She found a temporary secretarial job with the Manchester Chamber of Commerce and by the end of the year had relocated from London to Manchester. It is typical of a person who can leave no footprints that the Chamber of Commerce, despite exhaustive research, can find no record of Joanne ever working there. Staff, including Harry Potter fans, who have been working there for twenty years cannot remember ever meeting her. She also worked for a time at Manchester University.

But there was always the boy wizard to help while away the time and soon her notes on the saga filled a shoebox. Most authors say that this is the best fun in writing, running with the creative baton and seeing where it leads. Joanne had already decided there would be seven books, which some commentators thought arrogant of an unpublished author. But it was purely sensible – one book for each of Harry's years at Hogwarts. She had also settled on the name of her hero. 'Harry has always been my favourite boy's name and Potter was the surname of the family who used to live near me when I was seven. I always liked the name so I borrowed it.' Possible names for other characters would be collected enthusiastically and stored in the box: Dumbledore, for instance, is an Old English word for a bumblebee, and features in *The Mayor of Casterbridge* by Thomas Hardy.

Despite the almost Damascene vision of Harry Potter it was not the most significant event of the year. Anne Rowling died on 30 December 1990. She was forty-five. Joanne had been home to Church Cottage just before Christmas. 'She was extremely thin and looked exhausted. I don't know how I didn't realize how ill she was, except that I had watched her deteriorate for so long that the change, at the time, didn't seem so dramatic.' Joanne said goodbye to her mother, not realizing it was for the last time, on Christmas Eve and left Tutshill to celebrate the holiday with her boyfriend and his family. On New Year's Eve she was woken at 7.30 a.m. to be told her father was on the phone. That was unheard of and she immediately feared the worst. She instinctively knew what had happened: 'I still can't write about her without crying.'

Anne had died peacefully at home after a ten-year struggle against her illness. Pete Rowling, for the third time in his life, had to inform the registrar of a family death: his mother Kathleen, his father Ernie and now his wife Anne. Anne had never expressed a desire to be buried in the churchyard next door, preferring to be cremated. The simple service was held at the crematorium in Gloucester thirty miles away with just a few friends and the family present. Pete and the girls were driven there by Shirley Nettleship's former husband Peter, who had become a good friend. The late arrival of Anne's sister Marian and her husband Leslie was a further source of sadness. The couple had been held up in traffic due to an accident on the motorway. They arrived too late and the service had to proceed without them. Naturally, they were very upset.

Her mother's death had a profound effect on Joanne Rowling, one that she continues to acknowledge. It affected the direction of her own life and also the direction of Harry Potter. For a while she became rudderless. She returned miserably to Manchester, to a life that was going nowhere and a relationship that was deteriorating. After one particularly bad row she stormed out to a pub and later booked herself into a small hotel room in Didsbury, a suburb of Manchester.

The evening was not wasted. To take her mind off things Joanne decided it would be fun if they played a particular wizard sport at Hogwarts. She thought of Quidditch, an original game played with more than one ball and with a name which this time came from the recesses of Joanne's imagination and not from an atlas.

When Joanne was trying to think of a first name for young Master Dursley she originally thought of Didsbury, but in the end decided the residents of that Manchester suburb where she devised Quidditch did not deserve to be associated with Harry's ghastly relative. Wanting an alliterative name, Joanne settled on Dudley although only she could know what the people of that West Midlands town had done to warrant 'Dudders', as Aunt Marge calls him.

Joanne paid the best compliment she could to her mother by writing the chapter 'The Mirror of Erised' in the first Harry Potter book. It is probably the most famous of all Harry Potter chapters and the one of which Joanne says she is proudest. It is undoubtedly the most moving. The Mirror of Erised is a magical mirror in which the reflection you see is the image you most want to see in the whole world. Dumbledore explains to Harry, 'It shows us nothing more or less than the deepest, most desperate desire of our hearts.'

In Harry's case he sees his dead parents waving. His mother is smiling and crying at the same time: 'He had a powerful kind of ache inside him, half joy, half terrible sadness.' Joanne has admitted: 'When I reread the chapter I saw that I had given Harry lots of my own feelings about my own mother's death.'

If Joanne looked into the Mirror of Erised she would see her mother Anne. She revealed in a magazine interview that she would want five minutes to tell her all the news: 'I'd gabble on and at the end of five minutes I'd realize I hadn't asked what it's like to be dead. It's the selfishness of the child, isn't it?'

From the point of view of plot Harry Potter being an orphan is useful. He does not have parents interfering, he has to fend for himself and he can stay at school during the holiday breaks. To a certain extent Joanne felt that she had been orphaned after her mother died. Her feeling lent a more serious, moral side to Harry as a character. Those who knew Anne Rowling have spotted a debt to her in the first book. John Nettleship observes, 'When I read the books I feel I am always being presented with the values of Anne and Pete Rowling whose standards were very high. Both Joanne's parents had a strong sense of justice and a strong sense of accountability. I regarded them as being of the highest quality and what I love about the books is that they reflect the ethos of her family.

'You can see really that the books emanate from her childhood. It's not that they represent a sort of "I must write this in memory of my mother". It's nothing like that. Joanne has said that when she reread the first book she discovered there was a lot of her mother in that. This is what Shirley and I felt as soon as we read it. You're just aware of her mother in the background and the way her mother would think about things.'

One of the most obvious tributes to Joanne's mother is in the means by which the infant Harry is able to thwart the evil Voldemort. In *The Chamber of Secrets* Harry tells him: 'I know why you couldn't kill me. Because my mother died to save me.'

Shortly after the funeral, burglars broke into Joanne's Manchester flat and stole the few sentimental treasures her mother had left her. It was the last straw. She had never settled happily in Manchester and her university love affair had finally fizzled out. The time had come to move on.

CHAPTER SIX

Love in a Warm Climate

'I think Joanne was desperate for love.'

A SMALL ADVERTISEMENT in the *Guardian* news-paper caught Joanne's eye: 'Qualified English teachers required for a school in Porto'. Joanne had little relevant experience for a teaching job other than her year in Paris but Porto sounded just the sort of place where Jessica Mitford would have ended up. So she sent off a CV, a covering letter explaining her enthusiasm for teaching in Portugal and a contact phone number. The advertisement had been placed by Steve Cassidy, principal of the Encounter English Schools in Porto. The turnover of staff teaching English abroad was quite high, so every year he would seek to employ three or four new teachers, sifted from forty or so replies.

On a trip to England to visit his family in Darlington he would contact half a dozen appli-cants and arrange to see them. He met Joanne at a hotel close to the railway station in Leeds. 'We had coffee and chatted,' he recalls. 'She was a bit gothic-looking with very dark eye-shadow. She looked like Morticia from the Addams family. She wasn't an outstanding candidate but I thought she would be OK. She was a bit shy and I remember she looked a bit sad at the station. I think her mother had recently died.'

Joanne was told that she would be teaching English at all levels from beginners to A-level standard. Steve also told her a bit about Porto, although Joanne had already done some homework on Portugal's second largest city. The principal interest in the region as a tourist destination is the port wine. All the famous labels seen in wine shops and off licences are based here and Taylor's, Sandeman, Graham's, Offley and Cockburns open their lodges for tourings and tastings. Native citizens of Porto are fiercely proud of their heritage but that does not include port wine companies founded by English families. In fact Porto has acquired the sobriquet Invicta because the city has long refused even to have Portugal's king within its walls. One of the city's most famous sons is Henry the Navigator, grandson of John of Gaunt, who was responsible for many voyages of exploration to the West African coast in the fifteenth century. Ferdinand Magellan, leader of the first voyage to circumnavigate the globe, is said to have been born in the city but historians are not certain.

Joanne got the job. She was thrilled to be starting her own new adventure. Her father had begun to rebuild his life and moved from Church Cottage into a new home in Chepstow. Her sister Di was working as a nurse in Edinburgh. Joanne was leaving without regrets. She did not have many belongings to pack although the Harry Potter work-in-progress was not forgotten.

She caught the plane from Manchester on a dull, cold November morning and her first glimpse of a new home was when she looked out of the window to see the magnificent Rio Douro, the 'River of Gold' sweep into view. Porto has an awe-inspiring setting at the mouth of the river, which stretches west to the edge of the Atlantic Ocean. Steve Cassidy, who has the relaxed air of an Englishman abroad, was at the airport to meet her.

The drive into Porto is slightly less wonderful than the view from the air, combining heavy commuter traffic with unattractive industrial-looking buildings. On arrival in the city Joanne did not have to look for accommodation because Steve put up all the new teachers in a large four-bedroomed apartment above the Farmácia da Prelada on rua Central de Francos.

Fortunately for Joanne, excited but apprehensive, the other two new teachers and flatmates were also women in their mid-twenties with whom she had an instant rapport. Aine Kiely, a jolly Irish girl from Cork, and Jill Prewett, a more independent-minded English woman, became special and lasting friends. They were to offer Joanne invaluable support when her life became troubled in Porto. Indeed they are the subjects of a memorable dedication at the front of *The Prisoner of Azkaban*, the third Harry Potter volume: 'To Jill Prewett and Aine Kiely, the Godmothers of Swing.' This dedication, which has fooled many Harry Potter aficionados, has nothing to do with a love of swing music but is a tribute to the Saturday nights out enjoyed by three carefree young women in search of good times, good liquor and a little company.

Swing is a disco, one of the oldest in Portugal. Its unglamorous location next to a shopping centre, is away from the tourist areas along the Douro, at the top of the rua Júlio Dinis, a street named after the famous Porto-born author of *The Pupils of the Dean* and *An English Family*. There is a disco like Swing in many continental towns. The entrance is a discreet door at the end of a parade of shops. The downstairs area is a huge, dark, cavernous place with five bars playing British hits a fraction past their sell-by date. The clientele is late teens and early twenties, comprising mainly girls on the pull and macho Latin males trying to look cool. The three teachers were on the mature side for Swing – grandmothers rather than godmothers – but it was a fun place for them to let their hair down. The bar operated a system whereby the barman wrote down drinks orders on a special card, and the account had to be settled before the bouncers would allow revellers to leave at the end of the night or, more usually, in the small hours of the morning. Joanne quickly discovered that the nightlife of Porto did not get going until after 1 a.m.

The girls were befriended by Maria Inês Aguiar, a fiery, raven-haired woman who was assistant director of the Encounter English School. They would sit in the Confeitaria Labareda, a neighbourhood coffee shop and bar, a few doors down from the main school offices on the Avenida de Fernao Magalhaes (Ferdinand Magellan Avenue) and put the world to rights. Maria Inês would help them with their Portuguese although she does not remember Joanne being able to speak the language very well. She recalls, 'Joanne was a very nervous person, anxious and whirring around like a butterfly. She had this hysterical laugh which was a bit weird. I think she wasn't fulfilled. You could see that there was something missing. One day she even asked me to get her a boyfriend. I think Joanne was desperate for love.'

Maria Inês was to be an important figure in the remarkable course of events which were to change Joanne's life so dramatically, but that was more than eighteen months away. For the moment Joanne was settling into a continental way of life. Steve credits Porto with being a friendly city and one, which by English standards, is reasonably safe and secure for women. 'It may be a bit too quiet for some people,' he says, but that would not include those brought up in Tutshill next to a town without a cinema. The language school was a close-knit, friendly unit and the girls there played soccer in a five-a-side tournament. Joanne, notoriously bad at games, was relegated to chief cheerleader.

Homesickness at spending her first Christmas away from England was eased with a riotous Christmas party that Steve organized at a bar called Bonanza. Work was not particularly demanding. Steve observes, 'Aine was a brilliant teacher but Joanne was competent enough to do the job until the trouble started. She became emotional.' The main hours for classes were from 5 p.m. until 10 p.m. with a couple of hours on Saturday mornings, so there was plenty of time for her to shut the door of the computer room and type up her Harry Potter notes on a word processor. Both Steve and Maria Inês remember her as one of the fastest typists they had come across: 'She typed at the speed of light,' recalls Maria Inês. Joanne also spent many hours drawing and had become an accomplished sketcher with pen and ink.

During the day she could indulge her liking for writing in long hand in coffee bars. Porto is well served in this respect and one in particular, the Café Majestic on rua de Santa Catarina became a favourite haunt. The Majestic is a tranquil Art Deco oasis of style and flair with white marble table tops, ornate wooden chairs, chandeliers and a grand piano, which is occasionally played. Joanne could sit and smoke, sip her strong Portuguese coffee and dream of wizards. Porto is full of dark cafés where food can be purchased for next to nothing but the Majestic had elegance. It was a place where women could meet and talk and, crucially, not be bothered.

Most days Joanne would call in before work, then catch a bus up to the Encounter English School and type up her café notes before class.

For a change of scene there were the Palácio Cristal gardens, a beautiful stretch of parkland near the city centre where on warm days Joanne could sit under the trees with her cappuccino or, after a night out, a strong espresso, and watch the ducks on the ornamental lake or listen to the regal peacocks calling for attention.

Porto is an acquired taste. Steve Cassidy, who has lived there for twenty years and is married to a Portuguese woman, explains, 'It takes time to get to know Porto. When I first came here it was November and it rained for four months. Lisbon is obviously a beautiful city while Porto can appear a bit grey. But Porto has a great history.' There is a local saying: 'Coimbra studies, Braga prays, Lisbon shows off and Porto works.' But Porto does have romance in its heart, especially at night when moonlight picks out the pigeons flying around the church towers. And then there is the Ribeiro, the Riverside, the most beautiful area of the city, where Joanne, Aine and Jill would meet in the evenings for pizza and cheap wine and watch the sun set over the Douro. Maria Inês says simply, 'The Ribeiro inspires you.'

Whatever else Porto did for Joanne, it freed an emotional and volatile spirit which had been kept well hidden in the confines of Tutshill, the protected environment of Exeter University and the drab offices she had worked in before her Portuguese adventure.

The night that changed Joanne's life began in ordinary fashion. She strolled with Aine and Jill to the Labareda for an evening drink. It was a typical Saturday night in March and she had been in Porto for five months. The three friends decided to move on to the Ribeiro to a bar and perhaps a club. They chose the Meia Cava, a place where, according to Maria Inês, 'you could go crazy, get drunk and look for love'. It is a few yards back from the river in a little courtyard square littered with tables and chairs where friends and sweethearts unwind with coffee and beers. Meia Cava has a plain dark green door with no name on it. Downstairs was a mellow bar area with jazz music and upstairs a disco. Joanne and the 'godmothers' chose downstairs where, by chance, a young Portuguese journalism student was drinking with friends. 'This girl with the most amazing blue eyes walked in,' he remembers.

Jorge Arantes was unable to take his eyes off Joanne who, with her mane of dark red hair and deep eye-shadow, stood out as different from Portuguese girls. English girls were always a target for the good-looking local boys and for the athletic-looking Jorge, Joanne was no exception. Maria Inês explains it simply, 'Our men are macho and English girls are easy.' Joanne has never spoken of the passionate, mercurial affair which began that night but Jorge has spoken at length about it to

Dennis Rice of the *Daily Express* which bought his story after Joanne became famous.

They realized that evening there could be something more between them than a night of flirting in a bar because they shared a love of books. Although Joanne spoke practically no Portuguese, Jorge had a good command of English. At the time Joanne was rereading Jane Austen's *Sense and Sensibility*, one of her favourite books and one which Jorge had read; not many good-looking young Portuguese men out and about in the Ribeiro district that night could boast of that. Jorge recalled, 'We were very comfortable with each other and spoke for at least two hours. At the end of the evening we shared a kiss and exchanged telephone numbers.'

Jorge did not call straight away, not wishing to appear too keen. Instead he rang two days later and they arranged to go out that evening: 'Before we knew what was happening she was back at my flat and we spent the night together. There was nothing sordid about it; we were simply two young, independent people enjoying life.'

According to Jorge he received an insight into the type of relationship that would develop when he bumped into Joanne a few days later in another bar and she saw him talking to a Dutch girl. Joanne marched over to have a quiet word with her new lover: 'Jorge,' she whispered, 'if there is going to be anything between us I will not share you with anyone else.' Clearly Joanne was not prepared to be just another notch on this cavalheiro's belt. If Joanne displayed the signs of a jealous temperament in the early phases of their love affair, friends noticed that as time passed by the roles became reversed. It was always a tempestuous relationship.

Soon the young lovers were spending more nights together than apart. During the day Jorge would meet Joanne in the Café Majestic or the Confeitaria Labareda near to her work. He did not impress Steve Cassidy when he popped into the Encounter English building: 'I didn't like him when he came to the school. I didn't like his look. His aspect was rough.'

They talked about literature. Joanne invariably had *The Lord of the Rings* with her, which she had first read when she was nineteen but was one of the books she wanted to take to Portugal. Maria Inês confirms that she always had her copy with her and Jorge recalls that she could not put the book down. Jorge learnt of Harry Potter and read the bundle of handwritten notes and typed sheets that made up the first story. He has always been fulsome in his praise of Joanne's creation: 'It was obvious to me straight away that this was the work of a genius. I can still remember telling Joanne, "Whoa, I am in love with a great, great writer".'

He remembers that Joanne had decided even then on the structure for all seven books. Jorge, who harboured ambitions to be a writer himself, maintains he was the first person to read the Harry

Potter manuscript and that he made suggestions. But Joanne, in a rare outburst, declared: 'He had about as much input into Harry Potter as I had into *A Tale of Two Cities*.' He does have a clutch of about twenty handwritten sheets of paper, but all that proves is that Joanne left them behind. The likelihood is that they did at least talk about the project. After all they were soon living together, and it would be an odd relationship in which the couple did not discuss hopes, ambitions and matters close to their hearts. Maria Inês discerns the influence like this: 'The writing was in Joanne's head but Jorge gave her an impetus, a release from her unhappiness.'

In the Harry Potter stories so far there is no obvious Portuguese influence. The cobbled streets and little alleyways leading down to the Ribeiro are full of charming small shops rather like Diagon Alley. But then Exeter, too, has little alleyways all around the cathedral, which might be equally influential as a model. One of the more fascinating links between Portugal and Harry Potter is through the famous Portuguese poem *Pedra Filosofal* – Philosopher's Stone. It was written by António Gedeão, the pseudonym of Romulo de Carvaiho. A renowned teacher of physics and chemistry, whose work reflected a great understanding of life, he became one of Portugal's most acclaimed writers. *Pedra Filosofal* is his best-known poem and one that Jorge and every other Portuguese student would have known well, not least because the words were set to music in a song by Manuel Freire. The simple melody combined with Gedeão's beautiful words has remained popular since its release in 1970.

Pedra Filosofal is about the importance of dreaming – something to which Joanne could testify. In translation, which always loses a little, it begins,

> They don't know the dream
> Is a constant of life
> So concrete and definite
> As any other thing
> As this grey stone
> On which I sit and rest
> As this gentle stream . . .

The poem ends with the sentiment:

> They don't know, nor dream,
> That the dream commands life.
> That every time a man dreams
> The world jumps and advances
> As a coloured ball
> Between the hands of a child.

Joanne discovered she was pregnant. It was not the best time for the couple. Jorge had to do eight months' National Service in the Portuguese Army. The couple, who had been together only a short time, decided against a termination. They were living with Jorge's mother in a small, two-bedroomed ground-floor flat in a terraced house on the rua Duque de Saldanha, in a neighbourhood away from the tourist trail. The street runs downhill towards the river and number fifty-nine is near the bottom just before the road fans out into a square. In one corner is the cemetery, the Cemitério Prad Do Repouso. When there is a funeral the square is bumper-to-bumper with parked cars. At other times Joanne and Jorge could stroll across to the edge of the embankment and look down on the splendid view of the Douro or across the river to the town of Gaia. The street is one of those that sleeps lazily in the sun. The locals enjoy their beer and coffee in the Café Sanzale or the Petisquale Alexander. Across the road the only shop is a florist called Mimosa. An incongruously large Shell sign outside marks a small garage. To describe the area as a slum, as some English observers have done, is inaccurate and unfair. Maria Inês Aguiar observes, 'Duque de Saldanha is rough but it has a community feeling.'

Number fifty-nine is a three-storey building. Besides the two bedrooms in the Arantes' apartment, there was a living room and a small kitchen. It is not unusual for couples to live with one or the other's parents in Portugal. It makes economic sense. Jorge's elderly mother Marília Rodrigues welcomed Joanne: 'She was a lovely woman and I saw her as part of the family.' Marília, a gentle woman, spoke only a little English and spent much of her time in church every day. She had little in common with Joanne.

As Porto became unbearably hot in the summer of 1992, Joanne and Jorge planned a trip to England for a month when she could introduce him to her family and friends and give everyone her good news. That plan was ruined when she suffered a miscarriage, but Jorge maintained this sad event brought the couple closer together: 'We decided that when the time was right, we would try for another baby and also get married.' He proposed on 28 August 1992. He remembers the date perfectly because Joanne playfully mentioned it in a letter to him at his barracks: 'August 28 1992. Jorge Arantes asked Joanne Rowling to marry him, taking himself by surprise almost as much as her.'

At the same time cracks were appearing in the relationship and one dramatic row reveals how flawed it was even before they had a daughter together, and how turbulent it became. The couple were having an afternoon coffee in the Casa Imperio across the road from the language school. There was no warning of the drama that was about to unfold or what sparked it although Maria Inês comments, 'He was very possessive and jealous.'

An argument exploded into life. Maria Inês recalls that Jorge shoved Joanne, nothing more: 'He pushed her and she screamed.' Joanne ran into the street screaming and shouting pursued by a still irate Jorge. Maria Inês remembers, 'She ran into our building and up the stairs into Room Two. A big crowd gathered in the street because they thought he was going to do for her. He had that look.'

Steve Cassidy could not believe it when he arrived back at his language school to discover about a hundred people trying to get a look inside, listening to the intense scene unfolding within. Maria Inês was there, anxious but trying to help: 'It was like a scene out of *Romeo and Juliet*. He was shouting, "Joanne, forgive me. I love you." And she was crying and shouting back, "I love you Jorge."' Someone had called the police, worried for Joanne's safety, and two officers went into the school to diffuse the situation. It was a public revelation that Joanne was involved in a volatile and tempestuous relationship and it was not to improve, regardless of the fact that they were to marry and have a child together. Only Joanne and Jorge know how many more rows of this nature went on behind closed doors.

The wedding was a curious, subdued and unromantic affair. Jorge had taken leave from his National Service. There was to be no church ceremony. Just before 11 a.m. on 16 October the couple presented themselves at the civil register office. The building, officially called the Primeiro Conservatória do Registo Civil, is about a mile away from the Café Majestic, further up the rua de Santa Catarina. It has a faded, dusty elegance with ornate iron railings and a Portuguese flag on a large white flagpole declaring it to be a place of some importance.

Joanne wore a black jacket with a V neckline, a three-strand pearl necklace and a pair of dangly earrings. Her bushy dark red hair was up in a more formal style, although the eye makeup was still decidedly black. Jorge wore a black jacket over a red and white polka dot shirt with a white t-shirt underneath. Joanne's sister Di had travelled from Edinburgh with her boyfriend, a dark and handsome restaurant manager called Roger Moore. After the ceremony, in a large carpeted office with leather furniture, the newly-weds signed the marriage certificate. Roger signed as a witness. Joanne was twenty-seven and her husband just twenty-four.

The photographs taken afterwards tell their own story. Joanne, clutching a small bouquet, is gazing uncertainly into the camera. Jorge, apparently more relaxed, is smiling and has his hand resting casually on her shoulder. And that was it – hardly the sort of day a girl who loved *The Little White Horse* or the novels of Jane Austen would have dreamed about. Jessica Mitford might have approved of the informality and unstuffiness of it all; she did not care for tradition. Later that afternoon Joanne went to work and taught a class of students. There was no honeymoon.

Joanne has never spoken of her wedding day but, in *Harry Potter and the Prisoner of Azkaban*, Professor Trelawney tells Lavender Brown in the Divination class: 'That thing you are dreading – it will happen on Friday the sixteenth of October.' Later in the book it transpires that Lavender's rabbit has been killed by a fox on the very day

The marriage certificate of Jorge Arantes
and Joanne Rowling

predicted by the divination professor: 'The sixteenth of October! The thing you're dreading. It will happen on the sixteenth of October! Remember? She was right, she was right!'

In 1992, the sixteenth of October was a Friday. It was also Joanne's wedding day.

Within a few weeks Joanne was pregnant again. It was a fretful time because of her previous miscarriage, but the pregnancy proved undramatic. She spent more time than ever working on her Harry Potter notes and her friends at the Encounter English School noticed she was more isolated than before, often sitting in the local cafés by herself. During her pregnancy Joanne would listen to Tchaikovsky's violin concerto every day. She had given it to Jorge for his birthday. She selected this piece of music as the one above all others that she would take with her on *Desert Island Discs* because 'it's got this very strong association with my daughter'.

Worryingly, although pregnant, Joanne was losing weight – eleven kilograms in all – and Maria Inês believes the doctors were concerned about her. It may have been a product of the stress caused by the jealousy and arguments between herself and Jorge. His mother Marilia observed, 'They loved each other but they were very jealous of each other.' If Jorge went out drinking with friends he would expect Joanne to be waiting at home for him. On the other hand he was not at all happy if Joanne went out with Aine and Jill. According to Maria

Inês, 'They used to say to Joanne "leave him".'

Joanne's daughter was born on 27 July 1993 in the Maternidade Júlio Dinis nursing home after a seven-hour labour and her parents called her Jessica. Joanne described the birth as 'without doubt the best moment of my life'. A boy would have been called Harry. Joanne has said many times that she named her baby after Jessica Mitford. Jorge tells a different story. He says a boy would have been called Luis Vasco after the famous sixteenth-century Portuguese poet, Luis (Vaz) de Camões, and a girl Jessica Isabel after Jezebel from the Bible stories.

Joanne continued to lose weight after the birth and there were worries that she was becoming anorexic. Jorge had finished his National Service but did not have a job and Joanne had always been the main breadwinner. 'They were having big arguments,' recalls Maria Inês. The tension was not helped when Jessica was rushed to Hospital de Sao Joao (St John's Hospital) with a circulation problem in a toe. Maria Inês believes the baby had caught her toe in Joanne's hair, which had cut into it. Jessica was in hospital for almost a month and for a time there were concerns that she might lose the toe, but to everyone's relief she recovered.

By November the marriage had reached breaking point. One evening another row erupted which once again led to a scene of high drama in the street. According to an article subsequently published in the *Express*, Jorge claims he exploded because Joanne told him she no longer loved him: 'I had to drag her out of the house at five in the morning and I admit I slapped her very hard in the street,' he is quoted as saying. In other newspaper articles Jorge has denied hitting Joanne but said he just dragged her forcefully out of their home. Either way, on 17 November 1993 Joanne Rowling was homeless, in a foreign city, with just the clothes she stood up in, and her four-month old baby was in the same house as the man who had just thrown her out.

Aine and Jill were there to help their distraught friend. They called Maria Inês who, being Portuguese, might be able to help Joanne get Jessica back. There was no question that the marriage was terminally over. Maria Inês called a policeman friend of hers and they went back to the flat with Joanne the next morning.

She recalls, 'I phoned a lawyer who told me to "pick up the baby no matter what". Officially the police could not do anything but I convinced them to come with me. I thought they might frighten him.'

Jorge answered the door, which leads directly on to the street: 'He told me he didn't want to speak to me but I had my foot in the door so he could not close it. I thought we were going to be attacked by the neighbours. I could hear the baby crying inside. I kept saying to him, "Jorge, give me the baby, give me the baby." In the end he brought the baby to me. Poor guy.'

All Joanne wanted to do was get out of Porto as quickly as possible. But there were arrangements to be made. Maria Inês remembers feeding Jessica at the language school while Joanne was getting organized. And all the time Jorge was trying to find out where his wife and child were. She was not staying with Aine and Jill because Jorge knew where they lived, so she was with other friends he had not met. Eventually, two weeks after her world caved in, Joanne and Jessica left Porto for good.

The question is: how could all this have happened to a bright, intelligent, sociable young woman? How did she end up in a run-down street in a Portuguese city with a baby and a husband with whom she rowed constantly and who, it would appear, frightened her? Maria Inês believes Joanne was 'very confused' and 'wanted very much someone to love'. Certainly her mother's death had left a void in her life which could now be filled by her own daughter.

Today Maria Inês has second thoughts about the wisdom of her involvement, especially as Jorge has not seen his daughter for many years: 'I don't think he and Joanne had enough time together to build a bridge between the two cultures. Jorge was a typical Portuguese. He was a very intelligent guy but our men are macho. I am really sorry for what I have done to him.'

CHAPTER SEVEN

The Poverty Trap

'I never expected to mess up so badly.'

IN OCTOBER 1993 THE British Prime Minister John Major, addressing the Conservative Party Conference at Blackpool, blamed single parents for the breakdown in discipline among the nation's children. *The Times'* political commentator Simon Jenkins was unimpressed: 'The judgement that puts single parents beyond the pale of family life, implies that they are inadequate, somehow guilty, is an insult to thousands of parents, widowed as well as divorced, struggling to bring up their children conscientiously'. Mr Major's words were not the reassurance Joanne Rowling could have done with as, a few weeks later, she prepared to return to the country to try to pick up the pieces of her life.

Her only consolation after the horrible events on the rua Duque de Saldanha was that at least she had her four-month-old baby with her. Despite all that had happened and the hardship she has faced since, Joanne has never for a single second regretted the birth of her daughter. Jessica remains the biggest priority in her life and she freely admits, 'Jessica kept me going.'

Her plan was simple. First it was to escape from Porto with her daughter. This had been achieved. They would be a lot more secure in her home country than in Portugal, where she was unsure of how the law might work. She needed to find a place to live and, in the New Year, a job, ideally teaching. She had very little money, enough to rent somewhere for a couple of months. Her friends in London had moved on so she resolved to try her luck in Edinburgh where her sister Di had settled happily.

The obvious question to ask is why she did not stay with her father while she took stock, especially as Christmas was near? He had maintained a good job with Rolls-Royce and, bearing in mind how close the family had always been, it would seem the most natural course of action. But circumstances had changed. Pete Rowling had remarried at the age of forty-eight, little more than two years after Joanne's mother Anne had died. His new wife Janet Gallivan, eight years his junior, had been his secretary.

None of the Rowling family has ever spoken of a rift between father and daughters. He was not at Joanne and Jorge's wedding nor did he attend Di's wedding in Edinburgh. He himself married Janet in a quiet ceremony at Newport Register Office on 2 April 1993 while Joanne was in the middle of her pregnancy back in Porto. When the first Harry Potter book was published in 1997 it was dedicated to Jessica, Anne and Dianne. Her father was conspicuous by his absence.

After Joanne had become a celebrated author the newspapers aired rumours of a rift. The *Sunday Express* wrote of an 'unhappy family secret' in January 2001: 'Within a few months of his first wife Anne's death from multiple sclerosis, Mr Rowling and Janet Gallivan set up home together to the astonishment of their own families.' That home was a modest two bedroomed house on a new housing estate in Chepstow, a couple of miles from Church Cottage. Janet had left her husband and two sons behind in Bristol.

Pete Rowling has always kept his counsel on his new relationship, preferring to live his life quietly and in private. He still pops in to buy his meat from Geoff Roser in Tutshill but does not linger for a chat. Evidence of a rift is strictly circumstantial and in Pete's defence, if he needs one, his first wife Anne died at their family home after being ill for ten years. And he was always there for her. John Nettleship, who knew the Rowlings for many years, observes, 'Pete has had a terrible time. He has had to rebuild his life.' And Maria Inês Aguiar remembers distinctly the impression she received when Joanne was in Porto: 'Joanne liked her father very much.'

Joanne and Jessica took a train north to Edinburgh to be near her sister. Disappointingly she had missed Di's wedding on 3 September, the third Rowling family marriage within a year and the third at a register office. Di married Roger Moore at the St Andrew Registration Office, India Buildings, in Edinburgh with just a few friends for support. They had not bargained on having Joanne plus baby arrive on the doorstep of their apartment at 140 Marchmont Road two months later, but there has always been a close bond between the sisters.

Di has the happy knack of looking on the bright side and she would always encourage her sister, most importantly in the progress of Harry Potter. Joanne later recalled telling her sister about Harry for the first time while at Marchmont Road. She had left Porto with the first three chapters written and notes on the rest of the first book and many more ideas for the remainder of the series, including the conclusion. Di persuaded Joanne to let her see what she had written so far and was instantly hooked. 'It's possible if she had not laughed, I would have set the whole thing to one side,' admits Joanne, 'but Di did laugh.'

Despite that warm response there were greater priorities in Joanne's life than Harry Potter. After all, she had first thought of the young wizard three and a half years before and only had three completed chapters to show for it, so it could hardly be said to have filled every waking moment.

Joanne saw herself as an independent and well-educated woman who was not going to be a burden to her sister or friends. She moved into a depressing flat at 28 Gardner's Crescent, not far from Princes Street and the city centre. Her life was beginning to resemble the type of relentless misery that Thomas Hardy might have inflicted on Michael Henchard, the Mayor of Casterbridge or Tess of the d'Urbervilles. 'I never expected to mess up so badly that I would find myself in an unheated mouse-infested flat, looking after my daughter,' she told the *Guardian*. 'And I was angry because I felt that I was letting her down.'

To compound her misery Joanne had to face the nightmare of bureaucracy. On 21 December 1993, she found herself relating her unfortunate circumstances to the local office of the Department of Social Security. She had to fill in form upon form to claim income support and housing benefit. She described her ordeal with candour: 'You have to be interviewed and explain to a lot of strangers how you came to be penniless and the sole carer of your child. I know that nobody was setting out to make me feel humiliated and worthless, though that is exactly how I felt.'

The reward for this humiliation was £69 ($103.50) per week with which she was expected to feed and clothe herself and her baby and pay all the household bills. One of the Christmas presents Joanne received that year was an album by REM and she found herself playing their haunting song *Everybody Hurts* over and over again. Eventually she could stand the sound of mice behind the skirting board no longer and, swallowing her pride, she borrowed £600 ($900) from her 'foul weather friend' Séan Harris, one of a number of friends who continue to be close and loyal to Joanne. But her hopes that this would lead speedily to better living quarters for Jessica and herself were crushed by red tape. She rang a dozen or so letting agencies in Edinburgh seeking to rent a new apartment but each said no. Joanne recalled this problem when she announced her support for a charity for single-parent families: 'Flat, bored voices on the end of the telephone kept saying, "We don't rent to people on housing benefit, sorry".'

It seemed hopeless until one woman either took pity on her or agreed to show her some flats to shut her up. 'I saw a chink of light so I started talking so fast she couldn't get a word in edgeways,' Joanne recalled. That same afternoon she was shown and accepted the tenancy on a one-bedroomed un- furnished flat at number seven, South Lorne Place, Leith, which is the old port of Edinburgh. It was a start. Her sister and the couple of friends she had in Edinburgh lent her a few sticks of furniture, and she and Jessica moved into the block which would be their home for three years and would be the place where, on her kitchen table, she would finally finish the manuscript for *Harry Potter and the Philosopher's Stone*.

Leith is by no means the worst area of Edinburgh. If Joanne had been at the bottom of the council house waiting list she could have ended up in a bleak area like Muirhouse with the all-too-common urban problems of drugs and crime. When she settled in Leith the area was undergoing a facelift, particularly along the waterfront where new bistros and bars were opening. The Shore, as it is called, is now among the most fashionable parts of Edinburgh. That was just a mile from Joanne's new home but it might as well have been on Mars.

Joanne and Jessica lived on the ground floor of a modern block of eight flats spread over four storeys. When she stood at the entrance and looked to her left she could see an identical block of brown and grey. Straight ahead was the same view and again to the right. In the middle was a little piece of unkempt green with a brown varnished table and bench. It was somewhere to sit, but who would want to? Certainly not someone seeking inspiration for their book. The streets around were full of elderly people, old residents of Leith who now lived in sheltered housing, closely watched by the local council. Around the corner on Lorne Street was a lively primary school, which Jessica would be attending when she was five.

Once more Joanne was a prisoner, as she had been at other stages of her life, at Wyedean School or in the rua Duque de Saldanha. Night after night she would stay in by herself with her baby to care for and for company. Then, just when it could not get any worse, Jorge arrived from Porto. It was the last thing she needed. After Joanne had left him for good Jorge sought consolation in drugs.

Joanne was able to call on friends to keep him

away from her and Jessica while she went half a mile to Commercial Street and the offices of Blacklock Thorley, solicitors. She has never said how frightened she was of Jorge by now, but this was a drastic step by any standards. On 15 March 1994 she began proceedings for an Action of Interdict, the Scottish equivalent of a restraining order, to stop him coming near her. Her solicitors issued a writ on her behalf and an interim order was granted. This is a serious matter in Scotland especially if the 'pursuer' (Joanne) decided to take the matter to the stage where the interdict became permanent. The wording of Joanne's interdict against her husband prevented him 'from molesting, abusing her verbally, threatening her or putting her in a state of fear and alarm by using violence towards her anywhere within the sheriffdom of Edinburgh'.

Jorge had no choice but to return to Porto.

For her part Joanne found herself slipping deeper into a depression – not a flatness, or a sadness, or a sighing 'I'm feeling a bit down today', but a deep black hole of despair. The Dementors, which appear for the first time in *The Prisoner of Azkaban*, are the creative result from a period of her life which she said was the most unpleasant thing she had ever experienced: 'It is that absence of being able to envisage that you will ever be able to be cheerful again, the absence of hope, that very deadened feeling which is so very different from feeling sad.'

The Dementors are the prison guards of Azkaban and a metaphor for depression itself. In tandem with The Mirror of Erised they represent the most personal aspect of the Harry Potter books so far and may be part of the proof that it is Joanne Rowling herself who is Harry Potter. She may be Hermione Granger, school swot and know-all, but she is also Harry, a child who misses his mother, who hates being the object of attention and gossip and who crumbles in the presence of a Dementor. With a kiss from the gaping, shapeless hole of a mouth a Dementor will suck the happiness out of people and take their souls. Despite their grimness it is an amusing touch that the antidote to the dreadful feelings brought on by the Dementor is, as every woman knows, chocolate.

The relentlessly miserable days rolled one into the other. One of the worst was when she went to visit a friend of her sister's and saw the number of toys her son had. 'At that point, when I packed Jessica's toys away they fitted into a shoebox. I came home and cried my eyes out.' On another occasion Joanne's health visitor – a compulsory extra for a single mother on benefits – brought round a few second-hand toys for Jessica: a grubby old teddy bear, a little plastic house and a telephone that you pulled along with a piece of string. Joanne was so humiliated by this act of genuine kindness that she stuffed the toys into a black rubbish bag and left it on the street for the refuse collection. The streets of Leith were full of bin bags.

At least there was Leith Links, a large slice of open green, half a mile from South Lorne Place. Joanne could watch the other young mothers playing with their children on the brightly coloured swings and slides, a Noah's Ark and a mast for climbing which looked like a DNA model. A plaque incongruously declares this to be 'The Home of Golf'. In 1744 the first official rules were drawn up so that a tournament could be played on this parkland where there was a five-hole course with each hole of more than 400 yards in length. The Honourable Company of Edinburgh Golfers competed for a silver cup. These days the Links is used by people killing time: young mothers like Joanne keeping their children entertained, students reading or sunbathers with nothing to do.

Somehow, the first summer after leaving Porto, Joanne started slowly to turn things around. The changes that were happening were not all for the worse. On 10 August 1994 she filed for divorce. Perhaps nine months of counselling helped but for the first time since her flight back from Portugal she started to think of plans and fill her days with something more than Dementors. Her brother-in-law Roger had formed The Sint Partnership with a friend called Dougal McBride and they had bought a not terribly fashionable café called Nicolson's near the junction of South Bridge and the Royal Mile. It was to prove a purchase of some significance for Joanne. She still wanted to write Harry Potter and her desire to tell stories and be a professional writer was as strong as ever. The height of her ambition was to hand her credit card to someone in a shop and for them to tell her that she had written their favourite book, but it was never going to happen in South Lorne Place.

She needed somewhere to go where she would not feel lonely or isolated but would be in the company of people leading their own lives who would leave her alone to pursue her own. Coffee houses had been a source of inspiration since her days working in London and later in Porto, but on her less than meagre budget she could not afford to spend afternoons drinking cup after cup of designer coffee. Nicolson's was a godsend. It was in the family so the staff would be sympathetic to her nursing the same cup of coffee for an hour, sometimes two, at a time. Fate may have been giving her a sign because one street away from Nicolson's is a road called Potterrow.

Joanne would set off with Jessica in her buggy and walk the half-hour along Easter Road to the centre of town. If she was lucky Jessica would be asleep by the time they reached South Bridge. If she was still awake, then Joanne would wheel her up the Royal Mile past the exotically named lanes that looked down on the rooftops of houses below. It is a very atmospheric part of the city and relatively unspoilt despite the bagpipe music that fills the air in this tourist trap part of town. Many places could claim inspiration for Diagon Alley, the shopping street for wizards in the Harry Potter stories. But few have a better case than Old Assembly Close, Anchor Close, Old Stamp Office Close and the many other narrow passages of Edinburgh's old town.

When Jessica was soundly asleep Joanne would walk over to Nicolson's and struggle up the twenty steps to the first floor and try to find a quiet corner table to work on her Harry Potter notes. Nicolson's had a cheap and cheerful studenty feel to it with a blue and yellow colour scheme, a selection of Matisse prints on the wall and distinctive Art Deco windows and lighting. Ideally Jessica would stay asleep while Joanne worked. At least in Nicolson's it felt as if she had a life. One afternoon a week a girlfriend would take Jessica for a couple of hours, and Joanne would be able to have a break, read a novel – she liked Nabokov and Roddy Doyle – or work on the rules of Quidditch.

Roger Moore, who, with his long dark hair looks more like a cavalier than a restaurateur, has never let on that they are related, preferring to create the illusion that his wife's sister was just another customer of Nicolson's: 'We all knew she was writing a book. She was quite often in several times a week, a good few hours at a time, sat drinking coffee. When you have a customer that's in for long periods of time, the staff soon get to know them and get to know what they're up to and why they're here. She got to know a few of the staff quite well, I think.' His business partner Dougal McBride remembered that Joanne would write everything in longhand: 'It was pen and paper, and scribblings out and looking through, just going over and over it.' Another member of staff recalled, 'The wee girl would sleep while her mother wrote.'

Joanne's patronage of Nicolson's has become a sort of legend – how she wrote with one hand while rocking Jessica to sleep with the other and how she chose to work on her book there because she could not afford to heat her flat in South Lorne Place. She would later reveal on *Desert Island Discs* that the stories were 50 per cent true and 50 per cent fabrication: 'It's true that I wrote in cafés with my daughter sleeping beside me. That sounds very romantic but of course it's not at all romantic when you are living through it. The embroidery comes where they say, "well, her flat was unheated". I wasn't in search of warmth. I was just in search of good coffee frankly, and not having to interrupt the flow by getting up and making myself more coffee.' Most importantly, Nicolson's and other places she discovered like The Elephant Café on George IV Bridge lured Joanne out of her sparsely furnished apartment and meant that she could leave the Dementors behind.

Joanne found a little secretarial work towards the end of 1994 that brought in an extra £15 ($22.50) a week, which she discovered was all she was permitted to earn before the state started deducting the equivalent amount from her benefits. At least the money made a difference, not least in buying nappies for Jessica. She wanted to work more and asked her health visitor if she would be able to find a state nursery place for Jessica for one afternoon a week. She was told that only children at risk could be considered for places and that Jessica was 'too well looked after'. Once more she found herself trapped in a Catch-22 situation: she needed a job to afford private childcare but she could not get a job until she found childcare.

Every week, meanwhile, she still had to face the post office in Leith Walk where she had to go to cash her benefits' cheque. She has never forgotten the shame society inflicted on her and others by the process of handing a benefits book over the counter in full view of people who might have agreed with John Major. 'I don't know what all the old ladies behind me would say if they saw it – "scrounger", "layabout" and "burden on society".' It was hardly surprising that she added, 'By this time most of the pride had been squashed out of me.' She did, however, have her wits about her enough to renew her interim interdict against Jorge on 23 November 1994.

Joanne found that her experience of teaching in Portugal would not be enough to begin a career in education in Scotland. She needed a post-graduate certificate of education (PGCE) to obtain registra tion with the General Teaching Council in Scotland, which would enable her to teach in Scottish schools. She applied to take a PGCE in modern languages at Moray House in the city centre. It is now part of the University of Edinburgh but, when

Joanne applied, it came under the administration of Heriot-Watt University. She was one of 120 applicants summoned for a gruelling day-long interview that would prune the candidates to a quarter of that number.

The day consisted of a group task, a written piece of work, a session of teaching and an interview conducted in the foreign language being offered as the applicant's main subject. Joanne's was in French although she had back-ups in Portuguese and German. The interview at the end of January 1995 was for a place on the year-long course beginning the following August. To her delight she was accepted; her first real achievement since returning from Portugal. She still had to sort out childcare and a grant award but at twenty-nine she was at last making progress. One of Joanne's favourite expressions of wisdom is the Buddhist truth, 'Life is Suffering'. It proclaims that we must all suffer to grow. Spiritually, by this stage, Joanne must have been ten feet tall.

In the summer of 1995 Joanne was able to come off benefits for good. A friend she has never named gave her financial assistance with her childcare so that she could become a full-time student again and she also received a grant from the Scottish Office of Education and Industry. There was one thing to finalize before she could embark on the next stage of her life. On 26 June 1995 her interdict against Jorge Arantes became permanent. He had never formally entered the process and had never sought to defend the action, which was therefore not proven although the order was granted. To back up her application, Joanne was required to present two affidavits giving evidence of Jorge's behaviour. She gave one and the second was from an independent witness whose identity remains confidential. The burden of proof for a permanent order is difficult, so Joanne's case must have been a compelling one.

On the same day, 26 June 1995, her divorce became final. She was no longer Mrs Jorge Arantes.

CHAPTER EIGHT

A Little Bit of Help

*'You'll never make any money out
of children's books, Jo.'*

BYONY EVENS OPENED the mail in the offices of the
Christopher Little Literary Agency in Walham
Grove, Fulham. It was a freezing February morning
with nothing on the horizon to brighten the day.
An English graduate, Bryony had spent eighteen
months working in a pub and six months working
in telesales before taking a job as the agency's office
junior. She recalls, 'I was quite happy to take a job
that paid virtually nothing in order to break into
publishing. I couldn't type but I was happy to do
the filing and learn as I went along.' That had been
eighteen months before and Bryony had since been
promoted to office manager and Christopher's
personal assistant. But she still had to open the
morning post.

Fortunately for Joanne Rowling, Bryony loved to
read, especially classic children's literature. She
thought *The Little White Horse* was a 'fab' book and
was a devoted fan of *Swallows and Amazons*, *The
Lord of the Rings* and assorted adventure and

151

boarding school stories. If Joanne could have handpicked someone to look at Harry Potter, then she could have done no better than Bryony who, at twenty-five, was the same age Joanne had been when she first thought up the schoolboy wizard.

The majority of the submitted scripts would go straight into the reject basket and that was where Harry Potter first went on that February morning. It was not because Bryony did not care for the manuscript. *Harry Potter and the Philosopher's Stone* was obviously a children's book and the agency did not handle them. Christopher did not think children's books made any money. 'There would be no point in showing something to Chris if we didn't deal with it anyway,' explains Bryony. 'I always sorted out everything first into stuff we handled and stuff we didn't, like children's books and poetry.' The good news for Joanne was that Bryony always had a flick through the reject basket later before sorting out things for return. She noticed Harry Potter at lunchtime because of the unusual black plastic wallet Joanne had used.

'I fished it out to take a look. There was a synopsis and three sample chapters, which was what we asked to be sent in as standard. The first thing I noticed was that there were illustrations with it. There was one of Harry standing by the fireplace in the Dursley's house with his scruffy hair and the lightning scar on his forehead. I started reading the first chapter and it was almost identical to how it was eventually published. The main thing that struck me, because I loved it, was the humour: when Mrs Dursley tells Mr Dursley that Dudley had learnt a new word "Shan't".' Bryony finished the first chapter and was sufficiently impressed to put the manuscript to one side to finish the remaining two later.

At the time the agency employed a young freelance reader, Fleur Howle, to look at unsolicited manuscripts and to work with authors on those they liked, to make sure they were of a high enough standard for submission to publishers. Fleur came into the office that afternoon and Bryony passed over Joanne's manuscript. 'This looks really good,' she said. 'I've read the first chapter and I'm going to read the rest later but do you want to read it now to see what you think?' Fleur read the whole submission and, like Bryony, was impressed. 'To be completely accurate,' recalls Bryony, 'I read the first chapter first and Fleur read chapters two and three first. At the end of the day I read them too and said to Chris "Can we send off for it?" and he said, "Yes, whatever." And that was it.'

Christopher Little is a man in his early sixties to whom the adjective 'clubbable' applies; charming and smartly dressed, usually in a pin-striped suit. But Christopher, who likes nothing better than watching a cricket Test Match at Lord's, is first and foremost a businessman with a practised eye on how to exploit fully every last ounce of potential from a project. He is a Yorkshireman by birth, which may account partly for his tenacity in business deals – a Rottweiler masquerading as a pedigree poodle. After a spell working for the Yorkshire woollen factories he spent many years in the shipping business in Hong Kong. When that took a turn for the worse in the late seventies he moved back to England where he started up a small recruitment agency in London called City Boys. He also began a small literary agency and ran the two businesses in tandem for ten years or so, until concentrating solely on the literary side. Not everything was a success, however, and grandiose plans to start a magazine called *By Royal Appointment*, aimed at royal warrant holders throughout Europe, fell by the wayside.

By 1996 his partner was the respected literary agent Patrick Walsh who had been steadily building up the client list over the previous four years. The two were very different characters but they gelled, probably because they were complete opposites. Bryony explains: 'Chris was a business-man first and foremost whereas Patrick was a literary agent first and foremost. But the two worked well together in that they could have arguments about stuff and one would bounce ideas off the other. Patrick would get his way in the literary side of things whereas Chris would hold sway over marketing. Patrick was very untidy and Chris was very neat.

'Chris was very involved in the promotional side of things. He was astute, for instance, in handling sports stars who wanted to do a book, like the

Olympic horsewoman Ginny Leng, because he could see the cross-media opportunities where you can get publicity for one venture through another. His was a business rather than solely literary approach.'

Up until taking on Joanne Rowling, the biggest name on the client list of the Christopher Little Literary Agency was probably the best-selling thriller writer A. J. Quinnell, coincidentally one of the few popular writers to use initials instead of a first name. A. J. Quinnell is a pseudonym used by one of Christopher's oldest and best friends who wrote his books in the Mediterranean sun on the island of Gozo, an existence far removed from the world of a trainee schoolma'am living in a one-bedroomed flat in Edinburgh. Quinnell's real name was Philip Nicholson but his identity was kept so secret that for many years A. J. Quinnell was thought to be a pseudonym for Little himself.

Crime thrillers were a special interest of the agency because it also handled the Alistair MacLean estate and books by Simon Gandolfi. Slightly less prestigious but highly lucrative was Anna Pasternak, the writer of *Princess in Love*, the book in which James Hewitt told all about his affair with Diana, Princess of Wales. Add to this list the doyen of royal writers James Whitaker, and Joanne Rowling was about to join an eclectic mix at an agency that was no stranger to very lucrative deals.

Joanne had found the agency in the *Writers' & Artists' Yearbook* in Edinburgh's Central Library and liked the name. It was the second London agent she tried. The first sent back a curt refusal and annoyed Joanne by not returning the special black file in which she had sent her work. Bryony wrote to Joanne on Christopher's behalf asking for the rest of the manuscript. 'It wasn't a priority or anything,' she recalls, but that was not how Joanne saw things back in her flat in South Lorne Place. She was dancing round the kitchen table. 'I assumed it was a rejection note but inside was a letter saying, "Thank you. We would be pleased to receive the balance of your manuscript on an exclusive basis." It was the best letter of my life. I read it eight times,' she said. The rest of *Harry Potter and the Philosopher's Stone* dropped on the mat in Walham Grove within a week, just in case Christopher Little should change his mind. Joanne wasn't to know that at this stage Christopher Little had yet to read a word of it.

That would soon change. Bryony, first of all, sped through the entire book: 'I read it rapidly because it was really good. I read it in a "I-can't-put-this-down sort of way". I gave it to Chris with my enthusiastic endorsement and he took it away and read it overnight. He would speed-read stuff but he always made a point of reading his author's material. To start with I wasn't convinced he'd actually read all of *The Philosopher's Stone* because he said he had read it overnight but of course when you think about it, you can read this book overnight.

'We discussed it the next morning and Chris was

very enthusiastic. There were only three or four things we wanted Jo to look at. I remember I wanted her to develop Neville Longbottom a little more. I thought he was such a lovely character. And Chris was very keen on the game of Quidditch, which he thought should play a bigger part. He thought it would not appeal to boys as a game unless the rules were in there. She had actually already written them so she just said "good" and put them back in. Jo had also enclosed an illustration of a Quidditch match; just a plain sheet of paper with the wizards on broomsticks interacting with each other.'

After three letters Bryony, who handled all the editorial communication with Joanne, was satisfied. She showed the manuscript to Patrick Walsh, who was as impressed as Christopher Little. At this point the manuscript was very similar to the one that was eventually published. Christopher is very careful about paperwork so an agency contract was despatched to South Lorne Place offering to represent Joanne under his usual terms: 15 per cent of gross earnings for the home UK market and 20 per cent for film, US and translation deals. It was a secure but standard contract from the point of view of the agency, binding Joanne to them for five years and then rolling on year by year with a three-month notice period of quitting. In effect it gave Christopher Little an agreement which could not be terminated until 2001.

Paragraph 1 of the standard agreement states:

'The Writer appoints the agent to be his/her sole and exclusive representative in all spheres of the Writer's literary engagements and literary activities including the writing of novels, short stories, plays, poems, film scripts, television scripts, songs, cartoons, articles and advertising and promotional material and the exploitation of so-called "merchandising rights" derived there from.' Nobody knew in the early months of 1996 just how big the merchandising of Harry Potter was going to be.

The punctilious Christopher Little included a letter drawing attention to the clause which states that the writer (Joanne) on the agent's recommendation should seek independent legal advice on the contents of this agreement to enable her to understand fully the terms and conditions hereof.

Joanne was thrilled beyond measure that a real agent was taking an interest in her book. She initialled each page of the contract as the letter requested her to do and returned one copy to the agency. The polite coda from Christopher Little that he 'looked forward to a long and successful business relationship' carried no more meaning than an epistolary courtesy. No one at the agency had any idea just how impoverished Joanne was. Even the postage was an expense that stretched the purse strings. And she would retype whole pages rather than indulge in the expense of photocopying. She was the poorest client Christopher Little had taken on.

It was time for *Harry Potter and the Philosopher's Stone* to be sent to a publisher. Bryony was in charge of sending it out. Christopher had told her not to spend too much on photocopying; it can get quite expensive copying a 200-page manuscript a dozen times. Bryony prepared three versions, put a new title page at the front and stamped each one 'Christopher Little Literary Agency'. The author's by-line was 'by Joanne Rowling'.

All Bryony could now do was sit and keep her fingers crossed. Penguin were the first to turn it down. At Transworld the woman who would normally have read it was off sick so it lay in a tray not getting read until Bryony asked for it back so she could send that copy out again. In all some twelve publishers turned down the chance to publish J. K. Rowling until a manuscript was sent to the offices of Bloomsbury in Soho Square. The publishing house had been set up in 1986 under the chairmanship of Nigel Newton and its biggest success until that moment had been *The English Patient* by Michael Ondaatje, which won the 1992 Booker Prize. Bloomsbury had recently started up a children's book division under Barry Cunningham, who had moved into editing from marketing and, like Christopher Little, had a flair for the business potential of a project.

Barry's ambition was to publish books which 'children would respond to' and he instantly found that quality in *The Philosopher's Stone*: 'It was just terribly exciting. What struck me first was that the book came with a fully imagined world. There was a complete sense of Jo knowing the characters and what would happen to them. It was, however, very long for a children's book at that time.'

The children's book division at Bloomsbury consisted of just four people: Barry, Eleanor Bagenal, Janet Hogarth and the publicist Rosamund de la Hey. They all played their part in the success of Harry Potter. Barry recalls how difficult it was to get his division's books noticed within the firm. It was Rosamund who hit upon the idea of attaching a tube of Smarties to the script when they sent it round to other editors there. The Smarties prize is one of the leading literary prizes for children's books. It is unusual in that it is partly voted for by children themselves and so is a more accurate reflection of what they are actually reading. In the future the Smarties Triple Gold Award would play a significant role in making Harry Potter a hot property.

Eventually, after about a month, Barry was able to make an offer of £1,500 ($2,250). Bryony recalls, 'I rang Harper-Collins, who had a copy of the manuscript, and told them that Bloomsbury were interested and asked, "What do you think?" They came back and said, "We really like it but we're not going to have enough time to put a bid together, so just go with the one you've got." So they dropped out, which left us with the Bloomsbury offer.' Christopher sorted out the finer points of the contract personally and advised Joanne to accept the offer.

Above and below: Joanne, wearing her favourite denim jacket and heavy eyeliner, socializes with new friends at the University of Exeter.

Above: Joanne wore black for her marriage to Jorge Arantes on 16 October 1992 and looks uncertain as she poses for a picture with her new husband and his family.

Below: A babe in arms: Joanne and Jorge relax with newborn baby Jessica.

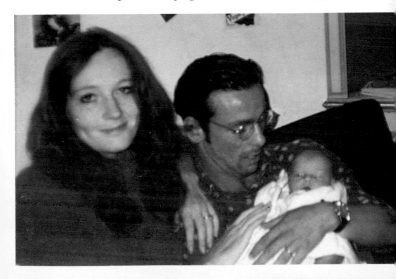

Right: Joanne spends an evening with her husband, Jorge, in a local bar in Porto.

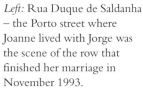

Left: Rua Duque de Saldanha – the Porto street where Joanne lived with Jorge was the scene of the row that finished her marriage in November 1993.

Above: In a rare family pose, Joanne embraces her father Pete and his second wife Janet following the ceremony at the University of Exeter at which she received an honorary doctorate.

Left: Joanne stands alone in her ceremonial robes after delivering a rousing speech to students.

Above: Joanne is most comfortable in the company of children, especially when promoting a good cause like the National Council for One Parent Families, to which she donated £500,000.

Above: After an extensive search, three children are chosen to bring the characters of Hermione, Harry and Ron to life in the film adaptation of J.K. Rowling's first novel: (left to right) Emma Watson, Daniel Radcliffe and Rupert Grint.

Above: While her baby daughter slept in her pram Joanne would drink coffee and work on her Harry Potter story in the soothing surroundings of Nicolson's in Edinburgh.

Above: Pottermania hits King's Cross station in London. As part of the promotion for her fourth book fans wave and cheer as J.K. Rowling leaves Platform 'Nine and Three-Quarters' on an old steam train.

Joanne Rowling proudly displays her OBE for services to children's literature after collecting the award from Prince Charles, a big fan of Harry Potter.

One of those involved remembers: 'Jo could not have been more delighted or grateful at the offer.' And so Bloomsbury secured the biggest phenomenon in modern literature for £1,500 ($2,250). It was a small fortune for Joanne Rowling, who would receive about £1,275 ($1,910) after the deduction of agent's commission. The money was paid in two halves, one immediately, the other on publication, scheduled for June of the following year, 1997. Bloomsbury made arrangements for Joanne to come to London and meet everyone for lunch. Joanne decided to travel to and from Edinburgh in a day because of Jessica, which meant sitting on a train for ten hours, but it gave her a chance to work on the second book. She was naturally nervous about her first steps into the serious world of publishing. She had not yet met Christopher Little or Barry Cunningham. One of the executives recalled: 'She was incredibly anxious in a fringe-in-front-of-your-eyes sort of way.' Joanne has never weaned herself off the student diet of cigarettes and caffeine, which is not exactly good for the nerves.

Lunch was at a little Soho brasserie, which gave Joanne the opportunity to pop into the famous Hamley's toy store in Regent Street to buy a present for Jessica. Barry Cunningham thought it a great lunch. 'I thought she was shy about herself but very confident and intense about the book and, most importantly, confident that children would like Harry. I knew she had had a tough time since coming back from Portugal so I was very impressed with her dedication to the story. She just so understood about growing up.' At the end of lunch Barry shook the hand of his latest author and told her, 'You'll never make any money out of children's books, Jo.' The remark has become one of Joanne's favourite stories.

At the end of a long day the future multi-millionairess clambered wearily onto a number one bus from Princes Street down Easter Road to Leith and home. Her one regret was that she did not meet Bryony, who had remained at Walham Grove looking after the office. Joanne thus missed thanking the woman who had made such an effort on her behalf and who was destined to leave the agency without ever having met her. Bryony had just moved house, started a new relationship and decided she wanted to earn more money. She worked for an estate agency for three years before starting work at the publishers Michael O'Mara Books.

Having only ever spoken on the telephone Joanne and Bryony finally met in October 1998 at the Cheltenham Literary Festival not long after the publication of *Harry Potter and the Chamber of Secrets*. Bryony went with her aunt and two 'borrowed' children to be in the audience of a question-and-answer session with J. K. Rowling. She recalls the day well: 'We were sitting in a corridor outside the room at about 10 o'clock when a woman clip-clopped past on very high heels. She was smartly dressed and quite little. I didn't like to say anything but I wondered if it was Joanne. Then we all went into the room and the children sat cross-legged around the platform, clutching their books, and the adults were in chairs behind them. Jo came in and did a reading and answered questions. She read the passage from the chapter in Book Two entitled 'Dobby's Warning' in which Harry discovers the house-elf Dobby sitting on his bed at number four, Privet Drive. Then the kids asked questions and I was surprised because they were all very intelligent ones from obvious devotees. They knew all about the books and were particularly interested in the names. We found out that Dumbledore was an old English word for bumblebee.

'I put my hand up to ask a question and she said, "Good, some adults putting their hands up." I asked her about the film rights: "I read you went with a lower deal because you wanted some control over it. Are you happy with the deal you've got?" She said she was and added, "I'm hoping to persuade Robbie Coltrane to play Hagrid but unfortunately one of the newspapers said Hagrid was a great big monster, which might put him off." I told her that the journalist who wrote the article obviously hadn't read the book and she was quite pleased at that.

'Afterwards there was a signing session in a marquee. My aunt had a copy of the adult edition of *The Philosopher's Stone*, which had just come out the previous week, and Jo told her, "This is the first one of these I have signed." I showed her a letter I had written about the book that had been published in the London *Evening Standard*. She saw my name and did a double take. Then she jumped up and gave me a huge hug in front of everyone, telling everyone who I was and what I had done for Harry Potter. It was lovely.'

HARRY POTTER

and the Goblet of Fire

Joanne has never forgotten the part Bryony played in her success and she was upset when a newspaper played down Bryony's significance in an article in July 2000 at the time of publication of *The Goblet of Fire*. When she saw Bryony again, on the day of the book's launch, she signed her copy with words to treasure: 'To Bryony – who really *did* discover Harry Potter . . . J. K. Rowling.'

CHAPTER NINE

The Prime of Miss Joanne Rowling

'Miss, are you a writer?'

NOT EVERYTHING WAS going so well for Joanne. The excitement of being taken on by a *bona fide* literary agency was tempered by a murderously hard term at Moray House. The second term is where the student teachers are subjected to what Joanne's tutor Richard Easton describes as 'hard-edged assessments'. For a start they have to star in their own video, which helps them to identify their areas of weakness and improve their technique for future job interviews. 'The students are under a lot of pressure in their second term,' he says. 'Everyone's got post-Christmas depression and the flu. By the end of the second term they're pretty well whacked.' This was certainly true for single parents and fledgling authors. Joanne had to do several weeks in a proper school where she was expected to start 'behaving like a real teacher'. She was placed in St David's Roman Catholic High School in Dalkeith, a small town on the A68 about eight miles south-east of Edinburgh. It meant a very long day, the only advantage being the location in a green area next to the Newbattle golf course and Benbucht Wood.

It was tough going for Joanne. She was assessed twice by a tutor from Moray House, Michael Lynch, who on the first occasion, on 19 February, gave her a D-grade, the minimum acceptable level, for her management of the class and planning of lessons. The management of a class included creating a 'purposeful, orderly and safe' environment of learning, managing pupil behaviour, sustaining pupil interest and motivation. Joanne's full grades were Subject and Content of Teaching D, Communication C, Methodology C, Management D, Assessment C, The School C and Professionalism B/C. Hermione Granger would have had a nervous breakdown.

Two observations from Mr Lynch gave cause for optimism, however. He thought she was very sympathetic to the needs of the pupils and that she collaborated well with other teachers. No one was expecting her to be a star teacher immediately but the assessment was a warning that she needed to improve if she wanted to make the grade. It had the desired effect. On her next assessment, eight days later, everything was better. This time she was given B-grades throughout except for her knowledge of the school, and Mr Lynch did note that she was particularly strong in knowing how to use help and expertise within the school.

He also thought her good at planning a coherent teaching programme. The time that Joanne was putting in during the evenings when Jessica was asleep, carefully working out her next day's programme, was paying dividends. He made special mention of Joanne's interesting and novel ideas and again drew attention to her sympathetic understanding of the needs of pupils. The school also thought Joanne had improved considerably in the short time she had been with them, especially in the area of presentation. The assessment recognized her patience and understanding while expecting a certain standard of behaviour – echoes of her respected English teacher Lucy Shepherd and of her own mother Anne. The strengths Joanne brought to teaching were evidently the same ones she brought to writing: careful planning, an understanding of children and what they like, and sackloads of imagination.

Summer term was still to come but, if Joanne could maintain this level of progress, then her teaching career looked every bit as promising as her writing ambitions. This time her placement of six weeks was more convenient, at Leith Academy, no more than 600 yards from her home. Opened in 1991, the Academy, which has a thousand pupils, is an amazing modern architectural specimen just off Easter Road. It is like a giant greenhouse full of labyrinthine passages bounded by exotic palms and ferns – a quantum leap from the wooden desks, inkwells and chalky blackboards of traditional schools. Most importantly for Joanne, it had a crèche for the children of staff and mature students.

As a student teacher Joanne came into her own at Leith Academy. She liked the pupils and she liked the teachers. Her supervising teacher Eliane Whitelaw was impressed: 'She had some of my classes and was very good. She was very organized and professional but also had a very good relationship with the kids. She was a very good person in the classroom.' The French classrooms were light and airy and Joanne's looked out on to a small green area, which was much better than many urban schools enjoyed.

Joanne was meticulous about preparing lessons. She had to teach all ages from twelve to eighteen and was not afraid to introduce her own ideas into the lessons. There was none of 'Please turn to page 343 of your textbooks' about Joanne's methods. For one lesson she invented an ingenious card game which, while not rivalling Quidditch, revealed her potential as a teacher. She drew all the illustrations herself. It is a card game for two or three pupils at a time. The cards, which are all illustrated, are divided into two piles. The pupil whose turn it is takes a card from each pile and has to make a sentence from the two objects on the card. The entire game is conducted in French and, if the pupil can make a sentence, he or she keeps the cards. If not, the cards go back to the bottom of the pile. It is then the turn of the next player.

In Joanne's model of the game Player A says

'Qu'est-ce qu'on t'a offert?' (What have you been given?) to Player B, who is selecting the cards. Player B then picks a picture of a jumper from one pile and of a grandmother from the other and says, *'Ma grandmère m'a offert un pull'* (My grandmother has given me a sweater), which is a good answer and he can keep the cards. He then asks Player C *'Qu'est-ce qu'on t'a offert?'* The game continues until all the cards are gone. The children of Leith responded well to Joanne's methods which were much more fun than sitting around asking *'Quelle heure est-il?'*

Joanne would also incorporate maps and diagrams, cryptic crossword clues, magazine articles from *Elle* and all sorts of her own illustrations. One task was for pupils to write a thank-you letter to a cousin called François who has sent a Christmas present. The pupils could decide what the present was but Joanne suggested some of the things they might like to put in the letter: *J'aime la couleur* (I like the colour), *merveilleux* (wonderful), *amusant* (fun), *je l'adore* (I love it). Joanne Rowling's lessons were very *amusant*. Richard Easton remembers, 'Joanne was very imaginative. I believe that's the most important quality a teacher can have. Some people teach from the textbook and that will be that, whereas somebody who has a bit of creative flair can come up with all sorts of interesting games. I remember Joanne's drawings. She was using her own skills and making them useful as a teaching material. That is the sort of thing we are most trying to encourage in student teachers. Many schools don't use textbooks and our teachers in Scotland are not tied to a national curriculum as they are in England. Our standard grade is the first set of national exams. The important difference in our system is that the means by which you arrive at that end point is a matter for you as a teacher.'

Eliane Whitelaw gave Joanne seven straight A-grades – a clean sweep of marks of an 'exceptionally high level'. She especially praised Joanne's ability to help pupils of different abilities. There was no dunces' row in Joanne's classroom. Eliane thought she created a very good working atmosphere in class and, crucially, helped pupils build up their own confidence and independence. As a teacher Joanne Rowling is the antithesis of Professor Snape of Hogwarts, who bullies and ridicules his pupils, especially poor Neville Longbottom.

Richard Easton visited the school and in his final assessment of Joanne before graduation high-lighted her planning, her communication skills and the level of pupil interest. He also made an observation that has subsequently been made about her time and again in the publishing world, that she had a high level of professionalism. 'It's a wee bit of a popular myth that she didn't spend time preparing classes as she should have done,' he explains. 'She maybe didn't spend as long as the other students but I think that was because she was using her time as effectively as possible.' In five short months Joanne had progressed from a D-grade student to an A-grade student. Aptly the school motto of Leith Academy is 'Persevere'.

Joanne graduated as a teacher in July 1996 and received her certificate in the McEwan Hall, one of the university buildings. To celebrate she joined her tutors and fellow students for a day out at Seacliff beach. The resort is notorious in history for the Witches of North Berwick. At Hallowe'en in 1590 witches of both sexes gathered at the Church of St Andrews under the leadership of 'the Devel' who in reality was Francis Stuart, Earl of Bothwell. He wanted to summon enough witchcraft to cause a storm in the Forth that would drown King James VI when he returned from Denmark. It failed to work but several of the witches were subsequently tortured, tried and executed for their endeavours. Historically wizardry and witchcraft is not all jolly broomsticks.

The students of Moray House enjoyed a fine day, swimming and a picnic. for Joanne a day at the seaside was rare indeed, especially one without Jessica. To end the evening in the best student manner, everyone went for a curry to the King's Balti in Buccleuch Street, south of the university. Richard Easton remembers having the longest discussion he had ever had with Joanne: 'She came up with these rather spiky comments and I said to her, "You don't have to be so defensive. No one's trying to do you down." And she replied, "I know. Sometimes I overreact a bit."'

By the end of this difficult academic year Joanne

had turned her life around. She was soon to be a published author, which was a dream come true even if she would not make any money out of it. And she had a piece of paper – a Post-Graduate Certificate of Education. She had a provisional registration for the General Teaching Council so that she could take a teaching post in Scotland. She could register as a supply teacher in Edinburgh and wait for a suitable opportunity to take a full-time post. She had started writing the second instalment of her Harry Potter saga using the Moray House computer room to type up her notes for the book that would become *Harry Potter and the Chamber of Secrets.* It beat working on her lesson plan.

Joanne was expecting to earn her living as a teacher. She had not endured the most difficult year of her life for her share of £1,500 ($2,250). Few things though are so exciting as waiting to see one's first book on sale in a bookstore for the first time. 'The purest, most unalloyed joy was when I finally knew it was going to be a book, a real book you could see sitting on the shelf of a bookshop,' Joanne remembers. But that was still a year away and she needed money to feed and clothe Jessica, especially now she was no longer on benefits. Supply teaching, replacing teachers who are off sick or away on secondment, was not well paid but it was better than the bad old days of sitting around the flat. Jessica was now three so Joanne was not yet concerned about her primary school, although there was one close by.

By happy chance she was given a posting at Leith Academy. It was the nearest school to her home and she had forged a friendship with Eliane Whitelaw. Although a fully qualified, experienced teacher Eliane was actually a year or two younger than Joanne. The two women would meet for coffee out of school hours and Eliane would help Joanne prepare her lessons. Leith Academy has a declared set of values for staff, pupils and parents which would not be out of place at Hogwarts: 'Success in learning for all; mutual respect and caring for others; individual needs and development; honesty and fairness in our actions.' One afternoon at Leith a girl turned up to Joanne's class with neither pen nor paper. Miss Rowling told her to fetch some from the teacher's desk. She told the *Guardian*, 'She was ages at the desk and I turned round and said, "Maggie will you come back and sit down?"' Maggie had discovered Joanne's secret among the papers on the desk and announced, 'Miss, are you a writer?' 'It's just a hobby,' mumbled Miss Rowling, embarrassed.

Richard Easton recalls bumping into her in the street in Edinburgh city centre and asking her how she was getting along. She told him that she had been writing a book in her brother-in-law's café and that it had been accepted for publication. This was a long time before the press took an interest in Nicolson's or its famous in-house author. Incidentally, Richard's recollections give the lie to the theory held in some quarters that Joanne's publishers as part of their marketing strategy somehow devised the story about the café.

Joanne needed to raise money. She was busy writing *Harry Potter and the Chamber of Secrets* and Christopher Little was encouraging her. But she and Jessica could not live on fresh air. The editing of the book had been painless. Bryony Evens remembers how struck she was, when the first book was published, by how lightly it had been edited. Barry Cunningham says they just 'honed' the manuscript. The famous opening paragraph, for instance, was just as Bryony first saw it. The biggest change was that Joanne Rowling was now J. K. Rowling. It was Christopher Little's strategy. He had consulted people in children's publishing and was told that, whereas girls would read books by male authors, boys would not pick up a book if the author was a woman. He told Joanne that it had to be initials plus surname. J. Rowling did not seem substantial enough, J. R. Rowling sounded like a character from *Dallas*, J. R. R. Rowling was verging on J. R. R. Tolkien, so after putting their heads together they came up with J. K. It flowed off the tongue, as two consecutive letters of the alphabet would, and Joanne liked the idea of adding her grandmother's name Kathleen to her own. The only problem was that she had to sit down at the kitchen table and practise her new signature. All her life she had signed herself either Joanne Rowling or just J. Rowling. Now she would have to master J. K. Rowling. She had no idea how many times she would be signing it.

Out of the blue Joanne heard of a bursary scheme for authors run by the Scottish Arts Council. The two conditions for eligibility were that you were resident in Scotland and that you were a published author. Strictly speaking, Joanne fulfilled only the first but was lucky to find a sympathetic ear in Jenny Brown, the literary director of the Council. She explains, 'We decided that Joanne would be eligible because she already had a contract with Bloomsbury. She wanted the grant to help her while she wrote the second Harry Potter book.'

Encouraged by Barry Cunningham, Joanne submitted a proposal describing what she was doing and why she needed the money, asking that the Council take into account her childcare costs and the fact that she had no current regular teaching work. Jenny asked Joanne to come for a preparatory interview at her office in Manor Place off Princes Street. Joanne told Jenny she intended to write a series of seven books. She had forty pages of *The Philosopher's Stone* with her and Jenny is delighted she was one of the first people to see part of the book. She was sufficiently impressed to put Joanne forward as one of forty applicants for the ten annual bursaries.

A special panel who did not need to meet Joanne in person reviewed her application. The next time she had news was when a letter arrived informing her she had been given the highest possible bursary award of £8,000 ($12,000). It was an early and encouraging indication of how her work would be received and was the biggest single sum of money Joanne had ever received. Coincidentally the next highest award of £7,000 ($10,500) went to Julie Bertagna, who has also become a successful writer of teenage books, including *Soundtrack*. Joanne has never forgotten the support she was given by Jenny and her team and she readily agreed to attend the launch the Council organized for a Braille version of *Harry Potter and the Philosopher's Stone*. She has subsequently won two Scottish Arts Council Book Awards and in 2001 gave back her £1,000 ($1,500) prize as a donation to help sponsorship of new writers. The bursary was another example of how Joanne's life was gathering momentum. It is a brilliant scheme and, unlike student loans, there is no condition to pay it back, not even for those selling 100 million copies of their books.

Each step Joanne took at this time was a positive one towards fulfilling her ambition to be a full-time writer. One of her first 'author perks' was being invited to a Bloomsbury roadshow at the Café Royal in Edinburgh where the publishers introduced their current crop of writers to important literary folk in Scotland. They had already sent out a manuscript to key sources including Lindsey Fraser, Executive Director of Scottish Book Trust, an organization that promotes reading through books. The Trust's brief is to recommend books which people, especially children, might enjoy. In the cutthroat world of publishing such an endorsement would be a great feather in the cap of an unpublished author. Lindsey's area of expertise was children's books, so she was a good barometer of how a new title might be received. She comments, 'I found it original, witty, ambitious and substantial. But I would never have thought things would have developed as they have.'

Joanne was introduced to Lindsey at a meeting that was to pay dividends a couple of years later when, as J. K. Rowling, she agreed to be interviewed for one of the *Telling Tales* series published by Egmont under their Mammoth imprint. These are basically informal chats with children's authors aimed at their principal readership. Lindsey had the advantage of being 'local' and of having written another of the series, *An Interview with Theresa Breslin*, author of *Kezzie* and *The Dream Master*. Lindsey says, 'I don't think Jo needed much persuasion to do the book because it was to be written for her readers and she always strikes me as very committed to them.' The end result is one of the most relaxed and informative interviews Joanne has given.

The first purchase Joanne made with her £8,000 ($12,000) grant was a word processor which would put an end to laboriously typing and retyping on the old second-hand typewriter. It would not put an end to writing in longhand in the corner of Nicolson's or some other Edinburgh coffee house. One of the things that is not generally realized about the Harry Potter series is that Joanne is writing all the books at the same time, in note form.

She plans histories for all the characters and, although they may not be needed in the books, she files them away using her foolproof system, a shoebox. Bryony Evens explains: 'She has to keep notes on everything for cross-referencing in a future book. In the first book, for instance, Hagrid drops off the baby Harry riding a motorbike lent to him by "young Sirius Black". Later on, in Book Three, we learn about Sirius Black and his motorbike, which he gives to Hagrid, and you remember when you first read about it. I don't know how she keeps track.'

Harry Potter and the Philosopher's Stone was published on 26 June 1997 in both hardback and paperback editions – seven long, hard years since he popped into Joanne's mind's eye on that train journey from Manchester to London. Finally her dream had been realized. The hardback print run was 500 copies. Barry Cunningham had commissioned the cover illustration personally. He wanted it to be approachable and charming – not too slick – but funny, reflecting the humour of Harry Potter. Thomas Taylor's illustration of a schoolboy with thick round glasses and lightning bolt down his forehead, standing in front of a bright crimson train bearing the sign Hogwarts Express, may rank as the most famous book jacket ever.

Joanne was so excited she spent the whole day walking around Edinburgh with the book tucked under her arm. She told Barry that it was like 'having a baby all over again'. She also told Lindsey Fraser that the first words Jessica spoke were 'Harry' and 'Potter' and that, without any pressure, she would shout them out in bookshops: 'I was sure people would think I was making her do it.'

There was no great fanfare to accompany the publication of the first book. The combination of unknown author and a plot involving a boarding school for wizards was not one likely to get literary editors buzzing with excitement. Barry had a very small budget – so small in fact he was unable to bid for US rights – and was unable to 'hype' the book at this stage. Instead he relied on contacting people he knew who might be sympathetic to the book. There was, however, an encouraging review in the *Scotsman*, which described it as 'an unassailable stand for the power of fresh, innovative story-telling in the face of formula horror and sickly romance'.

The *Sunday Times* also carried a favourable mention and importantly spotted that this was a 'funny, imaginative, magical story for anyone from ten to adulthood'. Ostensibly the target audience for Harry Potter was the nine to thirteen age group but Joanne was on the verge of a special break-through as a children's writer if her book could appeal to grown-ups. The newspaper summed up the plot: 'Harry Potter is deposited as a baby with dreadfully dull and unkind relatives for his own protection: he is the child of the wizard world. On his eleventh birthday, wizards come to claim him and train him for his destiny. This is a story full of surprises and jokes; comparisons with Dahl are, this time, justified.' Ironically Roald Dahl is not one of Joanne's favourite authors.

Within three days of the publication of *Harry Potter and the Philosopher's Stone* fate intervened in an extraordinary and totally unexpected manner. The phone rang at home at number seven, South Lorne Place. It was Christopher Little calling from New York explaining that there was an auction going on to buy the book rights for the American market and it sounded promising. Joanne later recalled in an interview in the on-line magazine *Salon:* 'An auction? I thought, "Sotheby's, Christie's? Antiques?" What is this all about? Then I realized that it was my book that was being auctioned off.' Christopher said he would keep Joanne informed. Behind the scenes the key figure was Arthur A. Levine, editorial director of Scholastic Books. By coincidence Janet Hogarth had left Bloomsbury to go and work at Scholastic and she nagged Levine to look at *The Philosopher's Stone.* He subsequently read it on a plane from New York to the Bologna Book Fair in Italy and had recognized an enormous potential for a US sale. He was not the only American buyer to be impressed but he was the only one to bid $100,000 (£66,666). He told the *New York Times,* 'It's a scary thing when you keep bidding and the stakes are getting higher and higher. It's one thing to say "I love this novel by this unknown woman in Scotland and I want to publish it". It's another thing as the bidding goes higher. Do you love it at $50,000? At $70,000?'

Fortunately for Joanne, Mr Levine loved it at $100,000 although he admitted he had never paid that much for a book before and that he was taking 'a great risk'. Even Christopher Little, calculating his 20 per cent, was less sanguine than usual when he called Joanne to inform her that Mr Levine of Scholastic Books was paying a six-figure sum for the book and would be ringing Joanne to congratulate her – in ten minutes. 'I nearly died,' she said. Mr Levine recalled, 'We had a very nice conversation. I said, "Don't be scared" and she said, "Thanks, I am." And we both said, now that we've paid this much, we had to concentrate on making the book work.'

This was a life-changing moment for Joanne Rowling. Looking back on that evening, in an article she wrote for the *Sunday Times*, Joanne recalled, 'I walked around the flat for hours in a kind of nervous frenzy, went to bed at 2 a.m. and was awoken by the telephone early next morning. It didn't stop ringing for a week.' The press know a good story when one smacks them in the eye and 'penniless single mother gets six-figure sum' was right up there with 'lottery winner can now afford life-saving operation for stricken child.' The broad outline of Joanne's life in Edinburgh was a publicity department's dream and deserved milking for all it was worth.

The newspapers loved it. The *Daily Mail*

declared: 'A penniless and newly-divorced mother has sold her first book for £100,000.' Joanne was not penniless as she had been given a bursary of £8,000 ($12,000) by the Scottish Arts Council; she had been divorced for almost exactly two years; and the book had been sold for $100,000, not £100,000. They were right about her being a mother though. Joanne's life was already being subjected to spin, simplifying the key events in her life and then exaggerating them. The newspapers quickly had the information that she wrote in a coffee bar while Jessica slept and that she lived in a freezing, grotty flat.

Would the Harry Potter phenomenon have taken off if Scholastic had paid a much less newsworthy sum for the book? Certainly the time and resources would not have been spent promoting it if they had paid, say, $5,000 (£3,333) for example. With so much money at stake, it *had* to succeed. Was the $100,000 well spent? Many so-called experts were doubtful at the first US print run of 50,000 copies, a very high figure for a first book. It entered the bestsellers' charts at number 135 but, just as in Britain, the popularity of the boy wizard spread quickly. By the end of 1999 Harry Potter books occupied three of the top four places in the bestseller lists of the year. It was the publishing equivalent of The Beatles.

Christopher Little told the press that the Scholastic deal was 'unprecedented' for a children's book. It was certainly impressive. To put it into context, Lynne Reid Banks had received

$670,000 (£446,666) for the sale of the American rights to her third teenage novel *The Secret of the Indian* when McIntosh and Otis sold it at auction in New York at the beginning of the 1990s. Joanne's deal was undoubtedly big for a previously unpublished children's author and big enough for the hype to begin.

Two weeks after the publication of *Harry Potter and the Philosopher's Stone* Joanne delivered the manuscript for the second volume of the boy wizard's adventures to her publisher. She had found it more difficult to write than the first, concerned that it might not be so well-received. She even persuaded Bloomsbury to let her have it back for six weeks so that she could tinker with the text. By now Barry Cunningham had left Bloomsbury. His agreement with the company had been for three years and he wanted to move to the country. He now runs his own firm called The Chicken House which publishes children's books both in the UK and the US. He remains very proud of his contribution to the Harry Potter story and of a book which would 'knock Hannibal Lecter off the top of the bestsellers' lists'. Soon after he left he attended a special day at a local school and noticed a young girl carrying a first edition of *The Philosopher's Stone:* 'I was curious to know what she thought of it so I asked her. I have never forgotten how she hugged the book to herself and said quietly "I love this book".'

Joanne has never forgotten Barry's contribution and has been very supportive of his new venture.

Meanwhile, the whirlwind that her life had become continued and she faced her first big exclusive interview with a national newspaper. Bloomsbury found a comfortable option for her interview in Nigel Reynolds, the urbane and witty arts columnist of the *Daily Telegraph*, the biggest selling broadsheet newspaper in the United Kingdom and Joanne, accompanied by Bloomsbury publicist (minder) Rebecca Wyatt, went to the *Telegraph* offices in London's Docklands. Reynolds liked her: 'We had a nice time. I remember telling her that in the future she would constantly be asked all these sorts of questions. She was a little bit anxious and she must have implied that she found it difficult because I told her that if all goes well then she would find her life becoming public property. She seemed as though she was worried about that. She was rather stern and worried.'

Nigel and Joanne chatted about the 'Pottered Biography' that was being made available to journalists during this publicity push by Bloomsbury. He observes, 'She gave the impression that she lived in a small dark flat and that she couldn't afford the heating. She confirmed everything we had been told. She and the PR seemed to have the story absolutely right. She talked about the baby in her carriage and the story we now all know came out. She also talked about the books as a series right from the start. She was also very guarded about her private life. She wouldn't, for instance, say anything at all about why she left Portugal.'

Reynolds was struck by her professionalism, even in her first faltering steps with the media, but he adds, 'She did not strike me as a happy person. Happiness was not a quality that shone through. I knew she had experienced a tough time in Scotland but she gave the impression of the world on her shoulders. Since then I have always felt that she was full of the sorrows of life.'

The *Telegraph*, understandably, wanted a photograph of her drinking a cup of coffee so everyone piled into a taxi and headed off to a street café in Covent Garden. Joanne, off guard and relaxing away from the newspaper office, was not the sleek, designer-clad figure who has looked resolutely miserable in a thousand pictures since. In the picture that accompanied the article she is very nearly smiling under her mop of dark red hair with the favoured look of one earring showing, dangling from her right ear. She was fortunate that in Nigel Reynolds she had discovered someone who could match her cigarette for cigarette and the pair puffed away happily for an hour over their cappuccinos.

As first interviews go it was relatively painless but Reynolds was right: Joanne has never enjoyed being subjected to public scrutiny. One of the few times she and Christopher Little came close to falling out was when he had agreed to a number of publicity commitments which she promptly cancelled when she found out about them. Exactly ten days after the publication of her first book Joanne was a page-three 'lead' in the *Telegraph*, an astonishing fillip for any burgeoning career, and the article was pretty much a blueprint for the perceived version of Joanne's life, the legend of J. K. Rowling: 'She would walk the streets pushing Jessica in a buggy until she fell asleep. She used to take the sleeping child to a café, order a coffee, spread her papers on the table and write feverishly until her child woke up.' The 'romance' of being a penniless divorcee hitting the jackpot did scant justice to the tough times through which Joanne had lived.

But the hype was effective. The next time Reynolds wrote about her was almost a year later when, six days after the publication of *Harry Potter and the Chamber of Secrets*, he reported that a children's book had topped a UK bestseller list for the first time. In both articles he mentioned that film companies were showing interest in Harry Potter. But the next important stop for Joanne Rowling was not Hollywood. It was number nineteen, Hazelbank Terrace.

CHAPTER TEN

On the Move

'I remember being struck by the totally easy way she was talking to her daughter.'

HARRY POTTER AND THE PHILOSOPHER'S STONE has been in the Booktrack bestseller list ever since its publication. It may not have enjoyed cult status to begin with but it sold 70,000 copies in the UK alone in its first year of publication and won the Smarties Prize for children's literature. But money from royalties is notoriously slow to find its way to the author. Joanne's first six-monthly royalty cheque was £800 ($1,200) with which she was absolutely delighted as 'she never expected to make any money out of it'. The second royalty cheque was for £2,000 ($3,000). So, by the time the second book *Harry Potter and the Chamber of Secrets* was the number one bestseller in the country, Joanne had earned a mere £2,800 ($4,200) in royalties.

The deal with Scholastic, however, was real money and Joanne knew the first thing she would do with her share: she would move from South Lorne Place. She had always been a little concerned about her security living there, and a broken window and attempted burglary made up her mind that she had to find a new home. Her sister Di, who had given up nursing to study law, was still living in Marchmont Road with her husband Roger, so Joanne began to look for a new home for herself and Jessica in streets that would be either a brisk walk or a five-minute taxi ride from her sister's flat. Joanne had never learned to drive but when her bank balance improved she could afford to take taxis around Edinburgh instead of walking or struggling on and off buses with her four-year-old. Her price ceiling was £40,000 ($60,000) but the most important criterion was finding somewhere near a primary school with a good reputation.

The Craiglockhart Primary School in Ashley Terrace was a good place from which to start looking. It is a few yards from the Lockhart Bridge, which overlooks the Union Canal, a lovely, tranquil place for a leisurely afternoon walk for a young mother and her child. Around two corners from the school Joanne discovered an apartment for sale in Hazelbank Terrace, a neat working-class street with a real community feel to it and children riding their bikes up and down the cul-de-sac. Joanne immediately took to it. The houses were small two-storey affairs with little front gardens edging on to the street. They would be considered ideal for first-time buyers. The neighbourhood was a pleasant mixture of residents who had lived in the same home for thirty years and more, and families with young children, most of whom went to

Craiglockhart. Joanne has not said where she thought up the name for Gilderoy Lockhart, the vain teacher who is one of her finest and funniest creations, but 'Lockhart' was a name she was to become familiar with on a daily basis.

Joanne shed no tears moving from Leith. In years to come she would be able to go back as a customer to any of the trendy restaurants and bistros along The Shore, establishments which up until now she had only ever walked past stopping to gaze at the menu a little jealously. She moved into Hazelbank Terrace in time for Jessica to start primary school in September 1998, shortly after her fifth birthday. At this stage nobody in the street or at the school realized that they had a best-selling author in their midst. Mothers who waited with Joanne at the school gates in the afternoon had no idea that the book their little one was clutching had been written by the woman who chatted away happily with them. One mother confessed that she would never have had the courage to speak to Joanne if she had realized she was J. K. Rowling. Joanne had been unprepared for fame and never welcomed its claustrophobic embrace. She told the *Sunday Times*, 'I had never expected anyone to be interested in me personally; my wildest fantasies hadn't gone much further than the book being published and the pinnacle of achievement seemed to me to be a review in a quality newspaper.'

Joanne's new home was on the upper floor of a house with its own separate red front door which opened immediately on to a flight of stairs leading up to two bedrooms, a kitchen and a sitting room. There was an attic conversion, which gave Joanne space to call an office for the first time, although Jessica would be playing Nintendo and other computer games there when she had the chance. Also for the first time Jessica could have her own bedroom.

The tiny front garden was paved, which suited Joanne who had not inherited her mother's love of gardening; her edgy temperament is not suited to such a calm pursuit. She did, however, give in to Jessica's pleading for a rabbit, buying one that she thought was a little dwarf bunny but which quickly grew into a lop-eared monster, always trying to bite lumps out of his owner. Later a guinea pig was acquired to keep it company. Almost every night William Ford, a neighbour, would hear the back door slam and Joanne shout, 'I forgot to feed the rabbit!' Appropriately Joanne also had a cat named Chaos.

Mr Ford was also slow to realize that Joanne was the author J. K. Rowling but, like the other neighbours, he did his best to respect her privacy. 'She was a very quiet person while she was here,' he recalls. 'We all looked out for the bairn. She was a wee one, Jessica, very small. Everyone looks after one another here.' Joanne became part of the community, even enlisting Mr Ford's help when she locked herself out.

Joanne was now a full-time author. She tried to

make life as normal as possible for Jessica even though she was now leaving home every so often for book tours and signings. She discovered that she had a great empathy with the children who came to see her or hear her give a reading: 'As a former teacher there is a blissful feeling of irresponsibility and knowing all you're supposed to do is entertain them and to hell with the discipline.' Also, as a former schoolmistress she did not appreciate the rudeness of two teachers who talked the whole way through a reading while sixty beautifully behaved children sat enraptured. The best moment for Joanne came on the tour to promote *Harry Potter and the Chamber of Secrets* in the UK. The mother of a dyslexic nine-year-old boy told Joanne that Harry Potter was the first book he had ever finished all by himself. His mother had burst into tears when she found her son reading the book by himself one morning after she had read aloud the first two chapters.

When the pupils of Craiglockhart school realized who she was, Joanne offered to give a reading so the children would stop pestering poor Jessica about her mother. 'It was the older children at her school who were a bit fazed because they were reading the book in their class,' Joanne says. Jessica, who made friends easily with the other young children at the school, had not read the books at first. Joanne had decided to leave it until she was seven but Jessica was getting so fed up with being cross-examined about Harry that eventually

Joanne, a little nervously, began reading the stories to her. Fortunately she loved them.

The more famous Joanne became, the more fiercely she protected her privacy. Occasionally she would pop into Margiotta, the delicatessen on Ashley Terrace about two hundred yards from home, but in the main she did her shopping in Stockbridge, a rather trendy area north of Princes Street and several miles from home. The literary agent Giles Gordon, who runs the Scottish office of Curtis Brown, recalls seeing a familiar face in front of him at the ham-and-cheese counter of a deli called Herbie's in Raeburn Place. She had a little girl with her and Giles recalls, 'She couldn't have looked happier.' When he reached the till he asked if that was who he thought it was. The assistant did not have a clue who he was talking about and when Giles suggested that she was in fact Edinburgh's most famous citizen he was told simply that she was a regular at the shop. Giles was so taken with the encounter that he wrote about it in his literary gossip column 'Agent Provocateur' in the *Edinburgh Evening News*: 'The salutary news,' he concluded, 'is that my children – who think J. K. Rowling is bigger than Shakespeare – will accompany me when I'm next off to buy eggs.' If they did they would not have caught a glimpse of Joanne. A few weeks later Giles was back at Herbie's: 'Thanks a lot,' they exclaimed. 'Ever since you wrote the piece, we haven't seen her. She was one of our best customers.'

It was further, light-hearted proof of how seriously Joanne Rowling takes her privacy. Another Edinburgh-based journalist is certain Joanne was in the habit of giving red herrings regarding the coffee bars she frequented so she would be left alone in the ones she actually used. She still went to Nicolson's but progressively less often as it became a key stop on the J. K. Rowling tourist trail. In any case in 1998 it underwent a comprehensive change, ditching the cheap and cheerful atmosphere that Joanne had found so conducive to writing, and became a plush restaurant with an adjoining bar area. Gone were the blue and yellow tablecloths and the Matisse prints and in their place were dark wood tables, claret seating, a wooden floor and modern minimalist decor. The management had decided to pitch for the young and trendy cocktail drinkers and the lucrative pre-theatre crowd popping over the road to the Festival Theatre. It was no longer a Harry Potter sort of place. One could not imagine a single mother on benefits sitting down, pen in hand, to enjoy a Tequila Mockingbird while her daughter slept peacefully beside her.

Coffee was not forgotten, however, and Joanne's brother-in-law Roger began a new venture called Black Medicine which aimed to open up coffee shops throughout the city to compete with other successful international coffee chains. He explained, 'We aim to create a warm and relaxed atmosphere by the extensive use of natural woods and exposed stone.' Coffee drinking has become inexplicably fashionable over the years and, in terms of the publicity Joanne has generated for Nicolson's, she has long repaid any debt to Roger and his staff. In years to come Nicolson's will no doubt feature in all the Edinburgh guidebooks as the place where J. K. Rowling wrote Harry Potter. There may well be a plaque on the wall outside. Small wonder then that when the Sint Partnership put Nicolson's up for sale in April 2001, the asking price was for offers over £325,000 ($487,500). But any future owners are unlikely to see much of J. K. Rowling – unless she is making a television documentary about her life.

The main impression that Giles Gordon had, standing behind Joanne in a deli checkout queue, was the rapport between mother and daughter: 'I remember being struck by the totally easy way she was talking to her daughter,' he says. 'It was very affectionate and down-to-earth. They were totally relaxed together and I thought there was a very good bond between them which I thought was awfully nice.'

Jessica, it seems, remains unfazed by her mother's fame. Joanne explained on *Desert Island Discs*, 'I think in one sense the blessing is that she was too young when it started, to really notice a difference. She's kind of grown up with this as the norm.' On one occasion Joanne tried to whip up a little bit of interest, turned on the radio and told her daughter that she was about to hear her mother talking about the book. Jessica was unimpressed: 'But I already know what you sound like, Mummy.'

So she does. Joanne has spent more time with her daughter during the early years than many mothers are able to and it shows. And still Jessica remains more important than Harry Potter in the life of J. K. Rowling: 'She knows, and she's right, that she's top dog.'

CHAPTER ELEVEN

Public Property

'Now I can't write!'

JOANNE'S WORST FEARS were confirmed on 14 November 1999. The newspapers had found out she was once Mrs Jorge Arantes. She had known that they would one day, but had never supposed that she would become so famous that they would be prepared to pay her ex-husband money to provide intimate details of their affair and marriage, for the titillation of several million people over breakfast. Ironically she had just been named Woman of the Year by *Glamour* magazine in America and, according to *Scotland on Sunday*, was Scotland's most eligible woman. Perhaps she was ripe for a media backlash.

Express Newspapers had agreed to pay Jorge £15,000 ($22,500) for a two-part series beginning in its Sunday paper *(Express on Sunday)*, and Dennis Rice was despatched to Porto to do the interview. At the same time Paul Henderson of the *Mail on Sunday* flew out in search of a 'spoiler', a story that would cost nothing but would steal their rival's

197

thunder. Dennis Rice was unimpressed by Joanne's ex-husband: 'I found him unpleasant. He didn't get out of bed until 2 p.m. I didn't want to spend time with him.'

The story was not difficult to assemble as Jorge spoke excellent English. It appeared under the head-line 'Lost Love Who First Saw Harry Potter'. The subsidiary headline was 'Ex-Husband Tells How Novelist Started Writing When She Became Pregnant', which was not true for a start. There was a picture of Joanne, Jorge and Jessica. In Jorge's defence he was gracious about Joanne in his story, praising her blue eyes. He was not vengeful. Even so, Joanne may not have particularly wanted the world to know the details of their tempestuous relationship.

The story trailed the second part 'In tomorrow's *Express:* Why I threw my wife out of our home five months after our baby was born and waved good-bye forever to our marriage and my daughter.'

Paul Henderson's story in the *Mail on Sunday* made her even more upset because it claimed Jorge had a hand in writing Harry Potter. He was quoted as saying: 'When I told Joanne to change something she would usually make the alteration. We read each other's work and made suggestions.' Henderson described Jorge as jobless and penniless after a less than distinguished career in local journalism, spends his days and nights in the dark behind drawn window shutters in a terraced house in Porto, wishing he had made more of his marriage to the acclaimed author.'

On the morning the stories appeared a friend rang Joanne. She recalled, 'I did not have a clue what had happened. He said, "Are you OK?" He was talking to me like I had just had major surgery. So I said, "Shouldn't I be OK?" He then said, "Oh my God, you don't know."' The poor friend did not want to be the one to break the news to Joanne and tried to ring off but eventually told her what was in the papers. 'All I could think of to say to him was "What *were* you doing reading the *Mail on Sunday*?"'

There was still the second part of the *Express* story to come. The revelations were more sensational. The article alleged that Jorge was now a drug addict. He was also quoted in the story as describing how he had dragged Joanne out of the house at five in the morning and 'slapped her very hard in the street'. Whether she read it herself or was told about it, the article would force Joanne to relive the worst times of her Porto adventure. At least Jessica aged only six could be kept in ignorance. She had better things to read.

Jorge claimed he just wanted to see his daughter again but failed to mention the permanent interdict against him in Edinburgh. He said, 'I do not want any of Rowling's money', although he did want the cheque for £15,000 ($22,500) from Express Newspapers. He did not get it. They claimed he had breached their exclusive contract with him because of the *Mail on Sunday* story and also another article in the Porto daily paper, the *Jornal de*

Notícias. So Jorge gained nothing from telling his story. He also revealed that he had met someone else: 'I cannot marry this other person until I can show that I am free.' New Register House in Edinburgh or Joanne's solicitors Blacklock Thorley, Commercial Street, Leith could have given him proof of his divorce on 26 June 1995.

For Joanne it actually could have been worse. There was no suggestion that she had been involved in a 'sex, drugs and rock 'n' roll' lifestyle, not exactly the right image for a children's author. Instead it was all very sad. As Dennis Rice observes, 'I think she has a strong sense of shame about the whole thing.' It is one thing the public knowing that you were once a 'penniless single mother' but quite another for everyone to read in the press that your ex-husband had kicked you out on the street.

From that moment Joanne has displayed a great mistrust of the press and an even greater desire to guard her privacy. More stories, some completely fabricated, began to appear and she told Ann Treneman of *The Times:* 'I was very vulnerable at that point. Then as usual, the worst sign that I am upset – and it really doesn't happen very often – I couldn't write. I went out that day to write. I went to a café and just sat there doodling. That made me even more depressed. I thought, now they've attacked the one thing that was really constant. Now I can't write!'

Joanne's remedy for her distress was not

chocolate but shopping. She went into a jeweller's in Princes Street, the main shopping parade in Edinburgh, and bought a large square-cut aquamarine ring without even asking the price. She had never been so extravagant and it could double as a knuckle-duster should the need ever arise again for Joanne to deal with a bully. 'You can't type with it on because it's so heavy,' she says. 'It's obscene! It's one of those things you have to bring out on certain occasions; it's not day-to-day because you could really hurt someone with it.' She also bought presents for some girlfriends and felt considerably better. It was just as well because, at the time, she was under great pressure to finish *Harry Potter and the Goblet of Fire* and was struggling with the storyline. Halfway through she noticed there was a flaw in the plot and had to begin again when she realized she had not set up the sequence of events that would allow the conclusion she wanted.

The newspapers' fascination with Joanne's former husband was not at an end. In the summer of 2000, two weeks before the publication of *Harry Potter and the Goblet of Fire*, he popped up again in the *Sunday Mirror* claiming she had virtually written *The Philosopher's Stone* while she was in Porto.

The article again made heavy reference to Jorge's alleged involvement in drugs. It did, however, report that he was making a fresh start [drug free] in the Clichy district of Paris. One month later he was talking to the *Daily Mail*, saying that he had decided to cut all ties with Jessica and Joanne. Again there was no mention of the interdict. He also claimed that Joanne left behind several manuscripts but he would never reveal their contents. The truth is that it scarcely matters. When Joanne left in such haste Jessica was – and has been ever after – more important than a few working notes. Jorge Arantes is simply part of Joanne Rowling's baggage of life and there is little she can do about the media pursuing figures from her past or present. For his part, perhaps Jorge too has now moved on with his life more positively, and is once again the charming man who so captivated Joanne.

In three years Joanne had become one of the richest and one of the most celebrated women in the world and it is a fact of celebrity that any chink of weakness is exploited to the full. The suggestion that her father had married his secretary with indecent haste, thus causing a family rift, was fully explored. Joanne is unusual in that she is a prime subject or target for both the serious broadsheets and the tabloid press. While the former are interested in her as a writer and literary phenomenon, the popular tabloids are more impressed by her celebrity status and wealth. Both are legitimate interests but, significantly, when she wanted to reach the widest possible audience on behalf of the National Council for One Parent Families, she told the story of her life in the benefits trap in Edinburgh to the *Sun*.

Whatever upsets her, Joanne has the satisfaction of being able to get her own back under cover of her books. She denies devising Rita Skeeter, the special correspondent of the *Daily Prophet*, as revenge against the journalists whose stories might have distressed her, and Rosamund de la Hey confirms that Rita 'definitely, definitely isn't' based on anyone in particular. Skeeter is one of the most glorious creations in the Harry Potter canon, the witch in magenta robes who uses a Quick-Quotes Quill to distort and make up quotes from her victims, Harry in particular. Joanne describes her with great relish: 'Her hair was set in elaborate and curiously rigid curls that contrasted oddly with her heavy-jawed face. She wore jewelled spectacles. The thick fingers, clutching her crocodile-skin handbag in two-inch nails, painted crimson.' When Harry responds to a question about the Triwizard Tournament with an 'Er-' the Quick-Quotes quill writes, 'An ugly scar, souvenir of a tragic past, disfigures the otherwise charming face of Harry Potter . . .'

Rita is a vehicle for a withering pastiche of tabloid journalism, remarkable from someone who has never worked on a newspaper. Joanne maintains that Ms Skeeter was originally destined for *The Philosopher's Stone*. When Harry first walked into the Leaky Cauldron she rushes up to him eager for an interview with the famous boy with the scar on his forehead. In the end Joanne cut her from the final draft in favour of an appearance in *The Goblet of Fire*. Joanne explained, 'I had planned seven books and the best time for her to arrive is bang centre in Book Four when the weight of Harry's fame really starts to oppress him.' Although she insists that the character is not based on any one journalist or influenced by one story, there is a similarity between the *Daily Record* story which claimed that Rowling had become 'reclusive, nervous and irascible' and a *Daily Prophet* exclusive which stated that Harry Potter had become 'unstable and possibly dangerous.'

The reporter on the *Daily Record*, however, can breathe a sigh of relief because *The Goblet of Fire* was written before her piece appeared. Rita finally gets her come-uppance when Hermione discovers she is an unregistered Animagus who can transform herself into a beetle and has been listening in on everyone's conversations to get her scoops. Hermione captures her in a glass jar. She does, however, live to fight another day in future books.

These days Joanne has enough influence to control much of what appears about her. The interviews she agrees to do are carefully chosen and planned like a military operation. One Scottish journalist explained, 'Arrangements are often very secretive. She is definitely becoming more accustomed to public life. She tends to discourage her publishers from overdoing things. Her preferred course of action to plug a book would be to sit in a hotel and see journalists all day, on the hour every hour.'

Gone are the days when she might pose drinking coffee in The Elephant Café or Nicolson's. Who needs to see another picture of Joanne Rowling drinking coffee? Those who have interviewed her have generally liked her for her sense of humour, her machine-gun laugh, her straightforwardness and her intelligence. And despite being the biggest star in modern literature she retains a sense of proportion. At the end of an interview with Simon Hattenstone of the *Guardian* she was persuaded to have a picture taken with a broom. She said, laughing, 'Let's be honest, I feel a twat about this.'

CHAPTER TWELVE

Hollywood

*'The picture has to be British and it has to be
true to the kids.'*

HOLLYWOOD CAME IN early for Harry Potter. First
out of the blocks was David Heyman, who had
moved back to London in January 1997 after
spending seventeen years in Los Angeles, first with
Warner Bros. and then as an independent producer
on films that included *Juice* and *The Daytrippers*,
which had been named best picture at the previous
year's Deauville Festival. He had also been
involved in the popular *A Little Princess* and knew
how to make a film appealing to a young audience.
More importantly he had signed a special first-look
deal with Warner to develop creative material and
identify potential co-productions through his own
company, Heyday Films.

Warner's president, Lorenzo di Bonaventura,
explained, 'Heyman will be our eyes and ears in
Great Britain. He will be our liaison between
England and the United States, helping to secure
financing for certain productions and developing
properties that could be produced more effectively

in the United Kingdom than in the US.'

Encouraging words for Mr Heyman but he still had to find a 'property'. Enter J. K. Rowling and *Harry Potter and the Philosopher's Stone*.

Tania Seghatchian, an executive at Heyday, was the first to read it and loved it. She told David about it so he read it and loved it. His children read it and they loved it. His friends had already read it and were most encouraging. He went to a dinner party at the home of publishing scout Koukla Maclehose and she also recommended it. Koukla is the London representative for a fleet of European publishers. She saw the potential of Harry Potter immediately and urged her friend Heyman as well as other clients to get his hands on it as soon as possible. At the time she had an au pair called Melinda, the daughter of Hungarian publisher, Istvan Balasz. Koukla told Melinda she should recommend *Harry Potter and the Philosopher's Stone* to her father. Istvan was initially unconvinced – the asking price was $500 (£333), a tidy sum in Hungary for an unknown author – but after much hesitation he took the book and published it under his Animus banner. After the publication of the fourth book *Harry Potter and the Goblet of Fire* Koukla asked Istvan how it was going. 'We have sold 60,000 copies so far,' he told her proudly.

David Heyman moved quickly to secure a personal option on the title but Christopher Little was not to be rushed. It would be a further two years before a deal was finalized with Warner Bros.

and by then the Harry Potter series were the biggest-selling books in the world and a far more valuable property. The remarkable thing is that so many publishers turned down the first book in manuscript and yet as soon as it was published there was a danger of being trampled to death in the stampede to secure a piece of the action. In an age of high-tech entertainment for children, the publishing world had underestimated the appeal of a traditional story, in which boarding school, orphanhood and magic combine to liberate the imagination.

David Heyman instantly recognized the visual possibilities of Joanne's extraordinary creation. He was not alone and Christopher was quick to exploit the interest. Nigel Reynolds in that first interview with Joanne ten days after publication wrote: 'Two Hollywood studios and an independent American producer are competing to buy the film rights.' The following day Tanya Thompson reported the same thing in the *Scotsman.* Christopher made sure everyone knew what a hot property he had on his hands. Joanne, in her 'grotty' flat in Edinburgh, was initially bemused by it all.

Joanne began to recover her confidence, restored by a combination of many things like being number one in the bestsellers' list, winning a prestigious book award, moving out of rented accommodation, seeing a crocodile of people queuing to meet her, or just simply signing a copy of her book. She was a successful writer. During the next couple of years

Joanne gained the strength and assurance to protect her creation and to take a professional interest in his development. There was no way, for instance, that Harry Potter would be attending the Beverly Hills School of Witchcraft and Wizardry. Joanne told the *New York Times*, 'I would do everything to prevent Harry from turning up on fast-food boxes. That would be my worst nightmare.'

The phenomenal appeal of Harry Potter in the US is difficult to explain. Joanne herself admits, 'They are such *British* books. There are no American characters and no American locations. I don't have an answer.' But she sees no need to compromise their integrity for the US market. 'You are not going to get an American exchange student brought in at Hogwarts. I don't think it would be faithful to the tone of the books to have somebody brought in from Texas or wherever it might be.' She had already won one battle with her US publishers who had wanted to change the word mum to 'mom'. But she did concede over the title of the first book across the Atlantic. It was felt that 'Philosopher' was not a word familiar to young Americans so 'Sorcerer' was chosen instead. As a result any Hollywood film would have to be called *Harry Potter and the Sorcerer's Stone* in the USA.

If you want to generate interest in a projected movie for kids then there are two magic words: the first is Steven and the second is Spielberg. As soon as he was mentioned in the same breath as Harry Potter, the movie world knew this was going to be a big film. Joanne was already indulging in that excellent dinner party game of trying to put actors to characters. She had always wanted Robbie Coltrane to play Hagrid, believing the actor, most famous for his role as the criminal analyst Cracker, could fill a screen in such a way that he was born to portray the Hogwarts' gamekeeper.

Towards the end of 1999 the film deal was completed. With all film projects it is very difficult to differentiate between hype and reality, fact and fiction. Christopher Little had brokered a deal with David Heyman and with Warner Bros. and Joanne was happy. It was not the biggest ever film deal, reported to be a million dollars, but Joanne had not sold Harry Potter down the river for three bags of silver. She would retain some say in what happened, would have some input into the script and had a veto on certain types of merchandising, particularly in Britain. In return Warner Bros. assumed worldwide control of Harry Potter as a brand, which she realized would mean clothes and games, drinks and chocolate, and big money. The columnist Libby Purves was already worried at the direction events were taking. She wrote in the *Times Educational Supplement:* 'Harry is going to get a baby blonde girlfriend and a mid-Atlantic accent. Eventually there will be theme parks with crooked little cute houses down Diagon Alley and games of virtual Quidditch on broomstick roundabouts.' She was understandably apprehensive for Harry Potter after what she called the disgraceful new ending tacked on the end of A *Little Princess* in which her father turns out not to be dead at all.

The first job for the studio was to appoint a director. Spielberg was the front-runner for a while but dropped out amid unsubstantiated rumours that he and Joanne did not see eye to eye about bringing Harry Potter to the screen. He moved on to another project for Warner Bros. A possible list of top-grade directors included Brad Silbering, Terry Gilliam, Jonathan Demme and Ivan Reitman. In the end Chris Columbus was signed on 27 March 2000, nearly three years after David Heyman first read Harry Potter. Columbus has an impressive track record, which includes *Home Alone* and *Mrs Doubtfire*, coincidentally from a novel *Madame Doubtfire* by Anne Fine that is set in Edinburgh. Perhaps more importantly he had been the screenwriter on successful children's fantasy adventure films like *Gremlins*, *The Goonies* and *Young Sherlock Holmes*.

Lorenzo di Bonaventura said, 'It was important to us to find a director who has an affinity for both children and magic.' Columbus, himself, did not waste time on media soundbites but was on a plane bound for London to meet Joanne for the first time. *Variety* reported that it was she and not the director or studio boss Alan Horne who would be the ultimate arbiter on the tone of the film. This may well have been the stumbling block over Spielberg's involvement. Joanne was already earning more money than she would ever need so throwing sackfuls of gold at her was not going to do the trick. She has always said that she wrote the books 'for me' and certainly not for Hollywood producers. She professed herself to be 'very happy' with Columbus as director.

This was never just a deal about one motion picture. From the outset Joanne has said that there would be seven books, so now there would be seven films. At this point the first three books had been in the top five bestseller list of the previous year and advance interest in the fourth was building to fever pitch.

The first task for the production team was to find a young actor to play Harry Potter. Soon the newspapers were full of stories of a 'big search for Potter look-alike'. The early favourite was Haley Joel Osment, who won great acclaim for his portrayal of the haunted boy in the Oscar-winning *The Sixth Sense*. He ruled himself out of the running because he thought the book should stay as a book and not be made into a film. Worried producers held auditions in schools up and down the country and encouraged interested children to contact them via the Warner Bros. website. David Heyman, by a lucky fluke, went to the theatre in the West End with a friend, literary agent Alan Radcliffe, who brought along his son who had recently started an acting career. David recalled, 'I was watching the play but the details melted into the background after I saw Dan. I called Alan the next day. I thought Dan so clearly embodied the spirit of Harry.'

At the end of August Warner Bros. announced that they had signed an eleven-year-old from Fulham in south-west London to play Harry. And when Daniel Radcliffe, with his wire-framed spectacles, was introduced to the press at a Knightsbridge hotel he looked uncannily as if he had stepped straight out of Thomas Taylor's illustration, like one of the moving characters in a painting at Hogwarts.

Daniel shyly admitted he had cried when he won the part. He is not, however, a newcomer to showbusiness. He had appeared on television in the BBC production of *David Copperfield* and made his film debut in *The Tailor of Panama*, the John Boorman adaptation of John Le Carré's bestseller which starred Geoffrey Rush and Pierce Brosnan – Daniel had played the 'tailor's' son. His father Alan had been an unremarkable actor before becoming a powerful literary agent with William Morris and later with ICM. His mother Marcia Gresham had also flirted with acting before becoming a respected casting agent. At least the new star had the right team behind him to negotiate a fee. He accepted a £200,000 ($300,000) deal for two films, which highlighted the dilemma Warner Bros. was facing: they had to put the second film into production before they knew if the first was a success. In the books Harry ages one year at a time and Daniel would need to do the same in the film.

Joanne was delighted at the choice of Daniel as she was with the ten-year-old Emma Watson and eleven-year-old Rupert Grint – a Potteresque name if ever there was one – to play Hermione and Ron. 'Having seen Dan Radcliffe's screen test, I don't think Chris Columbus could have found a better Harry,' she said. 'I wish Dan, Emma and Rupert the very best of luck and hope they have as much fun acting the first year of Hogwarts as I had writing it.' She told Chris Columbus she felt he had cast her 'long lost son'.

Both Heyman and Columbus were keen to allay fears that Harry Potter would become Americanized or Disneyfied. Heyman said, 'We have always been and continue to be devoted to remaining true and faithful to the books.' Columbus told *Salon*, the on-line magazine, 'The picture has to be British and it has to be true to the kids.' He added, 'At the first page, J. K. Rowling had me.' If he messed up her beloved book, J. K. Rowling was likely to have him by the throat.

One particularly cheery development was that Robbie Coltrane had signed to play Hagrid and that Dame Maggie Smith would take the role of Professor McGonagall – an inspired choice. With Alan Rickman as Snape, Richard Harris as Dumbledore, Julie Walters as Mrs Weasley and John Cleese as Nearly Headless Nick – on a reported £300,000 ($450,000) for three days' work – the film was beginning to resemble a Who's Who of British cinema. The screenwriter was Steve Kloves, whose credits included *The Fabulous Baker Boys* starring Michelle Pfeiffer, and he was happy for

Joanne to help with that side of things although by the middle of 2000 she was under pressure to publicize the fourth Harry Potter book. She did however have final approval on the script.

The next important part of the procedure was to find the right locations. Hogwarts and Harry's cupboard under the stairs were carefully recreated at Leavesden Studios, near Watford in Hertfordshire, but Joanne's flights of imagination did not make it easy. Despite lobbying from many tourist spots, Gloucester Cathedral was chosen as the main location for Hogwarts. Its atmospheric aspect had previously been used in the television adaptation of Joanna Trollope's novel *The Choir* and Dennis Potter's *Pennies from Heaven*. The Dean of Gloucester, the Very Rev. Nicholas Bury, was, like everyone else in the project, sworn to secrecy. 'Gloucester is one of the most beautiful and elegant cathedrals and the cloisters must rank among the most beautiful architectural gems in Europe,' he said proudly. Those cloisters, it was decided, would be perfect for the quadrangles of Hogwarts.

Other locations for parts of Hogwarts included Lacock Abbey in Wiltshire, Durham Cathedral and Whitby Abbey. The Australian High Commission in London doubles as Gringotts Bank. Warner Bros. was determined to keep as many locations as possible secret because they 'don't want people pointing at the screen and saying "Oh look, that's Oxford".' The place likely to become the most famous as a result of the film is the picturesque

Goathland steam railway station in the North Yorkshire village of the same name. It had already been used as a location in the popular television programme *Heartbeat* but for the film was transformed into Hogsmeade Station. In the book it does not have much of a billing, just a 'tiny, dark platform', from which Harry and his fellow pupils alight after their journey from King's Cross.

When filming began neither Daniel or Rupert had read all the books. Daniel confessed to having read the first two 'a long time ago' but he had completely forgotten about them. Child actors have by law to continue their studies, so a tutor travelled on location with them. Unfortunately for them the lessons were maths and 'Muggle' history and not Care of Magical Creatures. The bad English winter held up filming and shooting did not end on schedule in March 2001. This meant David Heyman had to apply to extend the length of the children's licences to miss school until July.

Making a film these days is only half the battle. The other half is the hype and publicity so that as many people as possible look forward to its release. That started on the first day of March with the release of a special trailer on the Warner Bros. website. It showed a montage of scenes including all the letters for Harry arriving down the fireplace, the train on its way to Hogwarts and Professor Flitwick's Charms lessons. And, of course, Robbie Coltrane as Hagrid.

There was a minor controversy when the *Sun* ran

a front-page story under the headline 'Harry Potter Drugs Shock' which turned out to be a lot less exciting than the shocking banner. Apparently some syringes had been found at Leavesden Studios and police had combed the buildings for more clues. It was a pity Voldemort was not arrested, but you can't have everything.

At the end of June more pictures from the movie were released including a shot of Fluffy, the three-headed monster dog who guards the Philosopher's Stone. Chris Columbus emerged again to reconfirm that he had not made another *Home Alone:* 'I promise, no. These books are incredibly imaginative, classic stories. Why would you need to toy with that?'

CHAPTER THIRTEEN

Honoris Causa

*'I was happier as an impoverished and
unpublished writer than I have ever been as a
solvent and mediocre executive.'*

JOANNE'S FOURTH ROYALTY cheque, two years after
the publication of *Harry Potter and the Philosopher's
Stone* had six noughts on the end. She was officially
a millionairess at the end of June 1999. From
cashing benefit cheques at the post office in Leith to
triple platinum credit cards had been a remarkable
five-year journey. By now Joanne had enough clout
to negotiate a very good deal for an author. She was
receiving royalties of 15–20 per cent on the cover
price of her books.

She and Jessica were still living in Hazelbank
Terrace. Her only ostensible extravagance was a
new fitted kitchen and the employment of an
American nanny to help look after Jessica. The
demands on Joanne's time were huge with
hundreds of letters to be opened every day and,
where possible, answered personally. She has
never forgotten her first fan letter from a girl called

218

Francesca Gray. It began 'Dear Sir', confirming that Christopher Little's strategy over her literary name was, at least initially, a success in confusing the reader as to the author's sex.

Life in Hazelbank Terrace remained quiet. Joanne has never been interested in becoming the great literary hostess of Edinburgh and is rarely sighted on the city's book scene. She may Apparate at the Edinburgh Book Festival in August but at no more than a couple of other events a year. And at home the occasional dinner party would be limited to her close and very loyal friends. On her kitchen wall she had pinned up the 'Dedicatory Ode' to Hilaire Belloc's *Verses* which she first read when she was ten years old and which says as much as anything about the way Joanne Rowling chooses to live her life:

> From quiet homes and first beginning,
> Out to the undiscovered ends,
> There's nothing worth the wear of winning,
> But laughter and the love of friends.

The residents of Hazelbank Terrace were proud of having a famous author in their street but were careful not to interfere in Joanne's life. She mixed easily with the parents of Jessica's friends but in protecting her privacy and Jessica's security was careful not to be too familiar with everyone. The street remained singularly unexciting, except when a car parked near number nineteen had all its wheels stolen. It was certainly safe enough for Jessica to ride her bicycle up and down. As William Ford observes, 'If she had been worried about security here she would have moved straight away.'

As it was, Joanne was seriously contemplating moving. It is, however, more difficult to pick up a millionaire's house in central Edinburgh than it is to find a two-bedroomed home. Joanne decided to take her time. In any case she was away a great deal on book tours after her third book *Harry Potter and the Prisoner of Azkaban* was published on 8 July 1999.

Its release marked her transformation, in the United States in particular, from popular author to superstar. Joanne has never forgotten arriving for a book signing at a store in Boston and seeing a queue that stretched for two blocks. Being British she naturally assumed it was for a sale, only to be told by the representatives of Scholastic that it was for her. She signed 1,400 books that day. One of the sales staff at the Politics and Prose store in Washington said of Joanne's signing, 'People started lining up early in the morning. It was like a Rolling Stones concert.' Strangely, book signings are not always great business for stores because devoted fans often turn up with books they have already bought and do not actually buy them on the day.

With her enormous American following came some unexpected but perhaps inevitable opposition from 'concerned parents'. At a special meeting, the South Carolina Board of Education was told, 'The books have a serious tone of death, hate, lack of respect and sheer evil.' Yet Joanne has always argued that Harry reflects the modern world because he is mixed race – his father a pure-born wizard, his mother a 'Muggle-born' witch. Arthur A. Levine of Scholastic commented that there were no plans to 'sanitize' Harry Potter.

In Australia, the Christian Outreach College, a private school in Queensland, banned the books from its library claiming they were violent and dangerous. A Christian Community Schools group thought the books should carry warning stickers about the danger of the occult, and the head of Cedar College in South Australia, Peter Thomson, declared, 'The books show occult as a really good thing and that's not a road we want to go down.'

Back in the United States an education expert claimed the books gave off the wrong signals to children by teaching them that boys were better than girls. Dr Elizabeth Heilman from Indiana said that Harry was always having to rescue Hermione from dangerous situations, making her out to be helpless. She thought the books showed girls to be 'giggly, emotional, gossipy and anti-intellectual' whereas boys are made out to be 'wiser, braver, and more intelligent and fun'. Yet Hermione is light years ahead of Harry and Ron when it comes to brainpower and has a better-defined sense of morality too. In each of the books she uses her indispensable intellectual abilities in support of

Harry and in the fight against evil. But as Joanne herself pointed out, 'My hero is a boy and, at the age he has been, girls simply do not figure that much. Increasingly they do. But, at eleven, I think it would be extremely contrived to throw in a couple of feisty, gorgeous, brilliant-at-maths and great-at-fixing cars girls.' But she does include three girls as the chasers in the Gryffindor house Quidditch team.

In the end a few 'outraged' opinions merely enhance Joanne's public profile rather than damage it and rally Harry Potter fans to his defence. There are plenty of them. The first three Harry Potter books had sold eight million copies in the United Kingdom and nearly twenty-four million in the United States by the time the fourth book was ready for publication. The US sale accounted for an astonishing 55 per cent of worldwide sales. The Harry Potter books are available in forty-eight languages around the globe and Christopher Little is confident that in the years ahead the foreign language sales will make up a far greater proportion of the total. Even China caught up with the activities of the schoolboy wizard in the summer of 2000 when the People's Literature Publishing House, which once issued the collected poems of Chairman Mao, released 600,000 boxed sets of translations of the first three Harry Potter books, the largest first printing of any fiction since the communists had come to power in 1942.

Reluctantly Joanne embarked on a series of 'big

interviews' which would whip up interest in the fourth book, *Harry Potter and the Goblet of Fire*. Never has there been so much newspaper space devoted to what a book might be called, as if the title would make the slightest difference to sales; the young world could hardly wait for its publication. 'Harry Potter and the Quidditch World Cup' was one suggestion that received wide circulation. And then there was the carefully leaked revelation that someone was going to die in Book Four. Shock! Surely it could not be Ron or Hermione? There was considerable anxiety among younger readers. It turned out to be Cedric Diggory who, until the fourth book, was not a major character. His death though, when it came, was none the less moving and upsetting.

The whole event was veiled in secrecy – a sure-fire way of fanning interest. The original manuscript was locked in a bank vault and no review copies were sent out. Joanne's editor at Bloomsbury, Emma Matthewson, was said to be terrified of muggers (not 'Muggles') who might steal the precious script. In the trade the book was referred to just by the codename Potter Four. One of the few people to have an advance copy of the book was Chris Columbus. He was honoured when Joanne gave it to him to read and he was unable even to show it to his children. They had to queue up for a copy like everyone else unaware that their own father had a copy locked away in his desk.

Bloomsbury allocated more than £2 million ($3

million) to publicize the book, a breathtaking amount. They failed miserably to generate interest. Instead they generated hysteria. The queues at stores on 8 July 2000 were of the sort one might have expected for a Beatles concert or for England in a World Cup final. And this was just to buy a book, not even to meet its author! There has never been a publishing event like it.

The figures alone are mind-boggling. By the publication date of 8 July 2000 the internet bookseller Amazon.com had taken advance sales of 290,000 copies. The average print run for a good selling children's book might be 20,000. The print run for the United Kingdom was more than a million copies. For the UK, Canada, Australia and the US together the figure was 5.3 million. Joanne was expected to earn £7 million ($10.5 million) from the sale of the first print run in the US alone. When the clock struck midnight in the US, 9,000 security trucks were despatched across the continent carrying the latest Harry Potter adventure.

In England Bloomsbury had hit upon a great wheeze – celebrating publication at King's Cross station. They made a mock-up of the famous Platform Nine and Three-Quarters. The day began at eleven o'clock which, as Potterphiles know, is the time the Hogwarts Express departs at the start of each term. And there was a special vintage train to take Joanne and invited guests on a trip into the countryside. In the event the occasion degenerated into bedlam, much to Joanne's embarrassment. An estimated 500 or more excited children had to play second fiddle to an army of press when Joanne finally arrived, in a turquoise Ford Anglia, of course. To her enormous regret she was unable to meet and talk to her real fans as the police tried to sort things out. It was pandemonium. The marketing people at Bloomsbury had done their job too well.

Amelia Hill wrote in the *Observer*. 'Two fathers, with weeping children clinging to their shoulders, bayed blue murder as they wrestled for a place near the crash barrier.' A parent complained, 'Where's the magic in this?' as her little boy whinged about the lack of owls flying about. The only people getting their books signed seemed to be the police, on duty to keep the peace, and the only ones having a conversation with Joanne were the press corps and the photographers shouting 'This way Joanne, look over here!'. The author, asked if she was amazed, replied, 'Think of a stronger word and double it.'

For her the children always come first and she was mortified. As the 'Hogwarts Express' departed all she could do was wind down the window and call 'I'm sorry!' to a group of disappointed children. Inevitably there was a backlash, noted by the novelist Penelope Lively in the *Independent:* 'As for reports of rioting parents at King's Cross, weeping children, bleary-eyed families keeping midnight vigils . . . enough is enough. Is this literary fervour or a lemming-like rush for the hyped trophy?'

The first thing everyone noticed about *Harry Potter and the Goblet of Fire* was that, at 636 pages, it was twice as long as its predecessors. Robert McCrum, literary editor of the *Observer* borrowed from Dorothy Parker when he said his first impression was that this was not a book to be put down lightly but to be 'hurled with some force to the corner of the room.' He also noted that it was a 'commercial blockbuster with knobs on'. Ms Lively thought the book too long and considered there was something formulaic in its structure: mysterious threat, trials to overcome, eventual triumph and revelation. She called for 'a more level-headed publication next time'.

Six days after the ordeal Joanne and her minders were on another train to the more peaceful ivory towers of the University of Exeter, her alma mater, where she had agreed to accept a degree of Doctor of Letters, *honoris causa*. The impetus for the award had come from Professor David Harvey of the Classics Department and his son Francis. Professor Harvey had become a great fan: 'I am sixty-one and I enjoy the books as much as children. She has an astonishing knack of telling a story and keeping it moving, keeping it funny.' He had been in touch with her after the publication of her first book and she had written a small piece for *Pegasus*, his department's magazine.

Joanne could hardly believe that thirteen years after leaving Exeter with an average 2.2 degree in

French she was back to be fêted in this manner. Glenda Jackson, a woman she admired because of her determination to change careers and succeed in a male-dominated world, was nearly fifty when she was honoured at Joanne's own degree ceremony in 1987. And here she was, Joanne Rowling, the undergraduate from Wyedean School, being celebrated two weeks before her thirty-fifth birthday.

One of the great things about universities is that time stands still for them. The student faces may change but often their clothes and style, their diet of cigarettes and coffee and their general demeanour does not. And the furniture of a university remains the same; that is the buildings and lecture rooms and, of course, the lecturers and tutors themselves. Nothing much had changed since Joanne had left; the manicured lawns and well-kept trees, the Northcott Theatre, the Devonshire House coffee bar all looked the same. So did the library, although it had changed its name. The original Arab donation for the Maktoum Library had long been spent. It was now plain New Library. Of the academic staff Joanne immediately recognized Martin Sorrell in the waiting processional line and ran up to him to say hello. She recalled the play *The Agricultural Cosmonaut* and chatted to him about the costumes. Martin was pleased she remembered him, as he had always liked Joanne Rowling the student. Best of all, her father Pete travelled from Chepstow with his second wife Janet and sat in the audience to watch his daughter, as proud as he had been when she first graduated. Any broken fences between father and daughter had been mended and he receives a dedication in her fourth book.

Graduation ceremonies are po-faced affairs. The academics and the bigwigs always look very serious in their exotically coloured robes. One could imagine that if one had a fit of the giggles the whole platform would shake with laughter at how *riddikulus* it all was. Joanne looked distinctly ill at ease. As an honours graduate she wore a vivid scarlet gown with 'spectrum blue facings and sleeve trimmings' over a plain black dress with smart black court shoes featuring a high heel so that she would not be incongruously small in the procession. Her hood was also scarlet, lined with dove grey and trimmed in spectrum blue. To top it off she had to wear a black velvet bonnet known as a pileus with a blue cord and a tassel. She had the air of a courtier in a Shakespeare play.

However she was feeling, she certainly looked nervous as she took her place in the procession. She was technically an honorary graduand until the Chancellor presented the certificate. The procession looked like a motley collection of birds of paradise. The Chancellor of the University, Lord Alexander of Weedon, wore a gown of black damask silk with gold facings and gold lace embroidery. His cap had a gold tassel.

The procession, led by the University Marshall,

followed by Joanne Rowling, entered the Great Hall at the back and walked solemnly through the assembled thousand or so undergraduates and proud parents to the stage. Then came the Dean of the Faculty of Postgraduate Studies, Dean of the Faculty of Undergraduate Studies, Dean of the Faculty of Academic Partnerships, Public Orator, Deputy Vice-Chancellor, Treasurer, Pro-Chancellor, Vice-Chancellor, the University Mace, Chancellor, Registrar and Secretary, Librarian and Chaplain. The solid silver University Mace is a symbol of royal authority that was quite apt on this occasion because one of the students receiving a degree was Peter Phillips, the son of the Princess Royal. He graduated with a BSc in Exercise and Sports Sciences.

The university librarian Alistair Patterson recalls Joanne shaking with nerves. He tried to put her at ease by talking about his first school, Leith Academy in Edinburgh, where Joanne had enjoyed teaching. Naturally shy, Joanne always finds it an ordeal to appear in public. She is happier with children. But in one way the honorary degree from Exeter was a fulfilment of the Hermione side of her nature, which had always sought academic approval. Her more immediate concern, however, was her pileus that was two sizes too big and kept threatening to slip down over her face.

The Public Orator is the member of the university's faculty who introduces the honorary graduand. In Joanne's case it was Dr Peter

Wiseman, a Professor of Classics. He began his address with a reference to *Harry Potter and the Goblet of Fire*: 'I have grave news. He Who Must Not Be Named has escaped from his living death in the forests of Albania . . .' It is testimony to the wide appeal of Harry Potter that the assembled academics did not think Dr Wiseman had gone mad. He went on to outline the public version of Joanne's life as had then been reported in newspapers and on the radio: 'The epitome of a bookish child – short and squat, in thick National Health glasses, living in a world of complete daydreams, writing stories endlessly.'

Dr Wiseman's genial account only scratched the surface but he did highlight the three important ingredients of her success: 'First, natural talent and the obsession to practise it – that daydreaming child and her stories. Second, formative experience – the bad times that strengthen the character that lives through them. And third, sheer hard work – a self-disciplined concentration, dedicated to achieving the end no matter'. Dr Wiseman's remarks recalled Joanne's favourite Buddhist truth of 'Life is Suffering' but they also included an often forgotten thought when considering her success: almost from the age that she could first talk Joanne Rowling was a storyteller.

Dr Wiseman also highlighted an important academic point: 'There are now 30 million or so people around the world who know at least one Latin sentence, even if it does mean "Never tickle a sleeping dragon,"' *(Draco Dormiens Nunquam Titillandus).*

The address was as light as a wafer but it did put Joanne more at ease. She came forward to applause to receive her certificate from Lord Alexander but she still had to wait to deliver her own speech until all the graduands had trooped up to the stage to receive their degree. The Sorting Hat would have had a breakdown at the sheer numbers. It brought back memories of her graduation when her name was read out '. . . *Timothy John Otway, Heather Jayne Reid, Joanne Rowling, Benjamin William Tarring . . .'*

Finally it was time for Joanne's speech and she has never delivered a better one. Rebecca Rampton, president of the Students' Guild, recalls, 'She gave the best speech I have ever heard. All the graduates in the audience could relate to it.' Joanne started by telling the audience about a congratulatory postcard which a contemporary from Exeter had sent her which said, 'I assume this is to show the new graduates that you can make something of your life even if you spend three years in The Black Horse.'

She had, though, decided to speak to them about three subjects that were dear to her heart: making mistakes, taking risks, and luck. She was disarmingly candid about her year of misery in Manchester, her mediocre ability at a succession of office jobs and her attempts to write an adult novel that proved to be very bad. Joanne revealed that she had a pronounced fear of failure when she left university: 'I was afraid to risk poverty and disillusionment and devote myself wholeheartedly to the only ambition I had ever had, to be a writer.'

Joanne admitted that it was only through her well-publicized period of poverty-stricken single parenthood that she found the courage to find out whether she had any true worth as a writer. Having no job, no money and no marriage meant there was absolutely nothing to lose. She admitted, 'I was happier as an impoverished and unpublished writer than I have ever been as a solvent and mediocre executive.'

The characteristics of natural humility and social conscience that so distinguish Joanne Rowling the person were apparent as she reminded her audience that they were lucky to be at this university because there were many people throughout the world with similar talents who would never have their opportunities. She reminded them that they were privileged people and that they should set about improving the world and not glorying in their own talents. It is an ethos she has followed herself with her patronage of several charities since she has met with success.

Finally, she told the students she hoped, 'that you will not be constrained by fear of failure, that you will not live up to any expectations but your own and that you find the work in which you can give of your best and therefore live the fullest and most satisfying life you can.'

It was rousing rhetoric and impressed the

students, who gave her a rapturous reception. Her father said that it had been a great day. Later Joanne was able to relax and mix with the faculty and others at a special dinner at the university. She never likes being on show. Now at least she could dispense with that *riddikulus* bonnet.

CHAPTER FOURTEEN

Sweet Charity

*'We have to fight twice as hard
to get half as far.'*

THE CONFIDENCE THAT Joanne now felt emboldened her to stand up and be counted on issues that were important to her. Now that she was a seriously rich and famous woman, however much she sought to avoid publicity, she had a public image that she could use to the advantage of others. As a result she is a strong supporter of three charities as well as providing what has been described as the biggest single donation to a charity – the royalties from two small books to Comic Relief.

Her first philanthropic act was to donate £500,000 ($750,000) to the National Council for One Parent Families based in London. She also accepted the post of ambassador for the charity in September 2000. Joanne always rages at the negative stereotyping of single parents and felt that she had to do something about it; now she had the chance. As helpful as her substantial donation was, the publicity she generated by writing a piece for the

Sun was just as important for the cause. She has always been a bit of a *Guardian* person, but recognized the value of the *Sun's* circulation of more than three million.

Her article was refreshingly frank and told how she had been trapped in a bureaucratic prison from which she was lucky to escape. Her candour about her past misfortune, rare in a celebrity, left the firm impression that she had grown stronger and more committed. The facts that emerged about single parents in the article made grim reading: 3 per cent of lone parents are teenagers; 60 per cent have been married and are now separated, divorced [like Joanne] or bereaved; nearly a quarter of British children live in a family headed by one parent; six out of ten British families headed by a single parent are living in poverty.

Joanne concluded, 'We are all doing two people's jobs single-handed before we even start looking for paid work and, as I found out the hard way, we have to fight twice as hard to get half as far.'

Closer to home, Joanne has given her support to the Maggie's Centres in Edinburgh, which offer counselling and support for cancer victims and their families. The centres try to offer the sort of help which hospitals have neither the time nor the resources to supply. Joanne, who became interested in the charity when a friend was diagnosed with breast cancer, has done a number of book readings across Scotland to raise funds towards opening new centres in Glasgow and Dundee.

The third charity is the MS Society Scotland, close to Joanne's heart because of the illness that afflicted her mother. Joanne is patron of the charity and has already carried out public engagements in that role. She opened a new £250,000 ($375,000) resource centre for sufferers in Aberdeen in April 2001 and declared, 'I look forward to the day when this kind of centre is the norm rather than the exception. The truth about the appalling poor quality of care available to people with MS only became clear to me after I had been in touch with the MS Society in Scotland, which makes me doubly proud to be its patron.' Astonishingly, Scotland has the highest incidence of MS in the world.

Once again Joanne brought her pen to the table, writing an exclusive article for *Scotland on Sunday* which subsequently appeared in the *Observer*. It was both moving and a call to arms. Joanne estimated that her mother saw a physiotherapist, someone to ease her suffering, fewer than ten times in the ten years she had the disease. Her mother was trapped in Church Cottage because she lived in the country and could not drive. The physiotherapist and the home-help stopped coming to the house even though her mother had to crawl upstairs because she could not walk. Joanne's indignation at the sufferings her mother had to endure was almost tangible and boiled into outrage.

One of the few drugs that might benefit an MS sufferer, beta-interferon, is woefully under-prescribed in Scotland. Joanne explained, 'In Finland 15 per cent of the MS population get it, in Germany and Italy 13 per cent, in France and Greece 12 per cent, in both the Irish Republic and Northern Ireland 8 per cent. In Scotland, the MS capital of the world, 2.4 per cent. You've got a better chance of being prescribed it in Turkey.'

The state support for MS in Scotland stood condemned. The cost to give beta-interferon to each of Scotland's 10,400 sufferers would be £7 million ($10.5 million) a year, approximately 0.1 per cent of the country's health service annual spend. Joanne's argument that support for MS sufferers was as 'woefully inadequate' today as it was ten years ago was underscored by the knowledge of what happened to her mother.

On a lighter note Joanne was asked by the writer Richard Curtis if she would like to participate in the 2001 Comic Relief, whose obviously light-hearted packaging conceals a serious charitable purpose. She agreed to write two little books, of forty pages each, which could be sold on the back of the Harry Potter bandwagon with all royalties, at least £2.00 ($3.00) from every copy sold, going to Comic Relief. The books were part of Harry's Hogwarts' reading list – *Fantastic Beasts & Where To Find Them* and *Quidditch Through the Ages* – and Joanne even appeared on *Blue Peter* to drum up interest. She enjoyed writing them but the whole exercise took her ever closer to a showbiz world.

Another organization that solicited help from Joanne was the Labour Party. Gordon Brown, the Chancellor, is a great admirer of hers and of how she has overcome adversity. He joined her on 5 December 2000 at the conference of the National Council for One Parent Families and they clearly hit it off. It was widely reported that he asked Joanne to endorse the Labour Party, but she has kept her own counsel on her political persuasions. As the columnist A. N. Wilson has said, 'Writers on the whole make awful chumps of themselves when straying into the field of politics.'

Joanne, however, does not pull her punches on social issues. Her first speech as ambassador for the National Council for One Parent Families included a broadside for the then shadow Home Secretary for suggesting that married couples were 'the norm'. Again highlighting the figures which reveal that a quarter of Britain's children are being brought up by single parents she declared, 'Ann Widdecombe, justifying her remarks against lone parents, told *Good Housekeeping magazine* that she feels society should have a "preferred norm".

'We may not be some people's preferred norm but we are here. We should judge how civilized a society is not by what it prefers to call normal but by how it treats its most vulnerable members. When you take poverty out of the equation, the vast majority from one-parent families do just as well as children from couple families.'

Joanne may not have accepted Mr Brown's invitation but she did agree to contribute to a book of short stories with a magic theme being compiled by his wife, Sarah Brown, in aid of the National Council for One Parent Families. Joanne has said her contribution will definitely not be Harry Potter. Perhaps this is the moment to dust off 'The Seven Cursed Diamonds'.

CHAPTER FIFTEEN

And the Winner is . . .

'I'm trying hard not to do a Gwyneth.'

MANY AWARDS have come Joanne's way since the summer of 1997. *Harry Potter and the Philosopher's Stone* won twenty-one in four years. She has been short-listed three times for the Carnegie Medal, the most prestigious accolade of children's literature. In January 2000 it was a big story when she *failed* to win the Whitbread Book Prize, which went instead to Seamus Heaney, the Irish Nobel Prize winner, for his acclaimed translation of the Anglo-Saxon epic poem *Beowulf*. The awards had already attracted controversy with the appointment of model Jerry Hall as one of the judges and the towering Texan was on hand to embrace the winner. Joanne did win the Whitbread Children's Book of the Year Award at the same ceremony, for *Harry Potter and the Prisoner of Azkaban*, but was not there to collect her prize because she had flu. The actor, novelist and raconteur Stephen Fry collected the prize on her behalf. They had become friends after he agreed to read the audio version of her books. The marathon Boxing Day broadcast of *Harry Potter and the Philosopher's Stone*, aired for eight continuous hours, reached an audience of 3.5 million.

The surprising thing was not that Joanne failed to win the Whitbread but that a children's book by an author of three years' standing was up for a prestigious prize alongside a Nobel Prize winner and one of the great names in modern literature. Bryony Evens recalls that from the outset at the Christopher Little Literary Agency, 'We didn't see it as solely children's literature. It was a damn good read whether it was for children or not. When Joanne first conceived the books she didn't see them as just for children.'

A week is a long time in influenza and literature, and nine days later Joanne was well enough to hear actor Tom Courtenay read out the name of the winner of the Author of the Year at the British Book Awards, the 'Nibbies', at the Grosvenor House Hotel in Park Lane, London. It was a pity he did not pronounce her name correctly. It is Rowling as in 'rolling pin', an old unloved playground nickname, not Rowling to rhyme with 'howling'. Joanne did not look entirely at ease in her black designer gown as she tottered up to the stage. The Nibbies are the literary equivalent of the Oscars and Joanne told the audience: 'I'm trying very hard not to do a Gwyneth [Paltrow] here . . . This is such an honour. Thank you. Thank you so much. I have to thank Bloomsbury, as ever; in particular Emma Matthewson and

Rosamund de la Hey. I'm so terrified. If you were all nine years old I'd feel so much more comfortable. Maximum Strength Lemsip as well, I would like to thank. I'm completely overwhelmed as you can tell. I'd like to congratulate Jacqueline Wilson, because that is a great book, and I'd just like to say the great thing about winning this is that neither of us has to be photographed next to Jerry Hall.'

Joanne's observation about being more comfortable in a room of nine-year-olds was absolutely truthful. She is always happier and more relaxed in the company of children. Parents who have taken their children to meet J. K. Rowling 'on tour' have often observed that she does not talk down to them but treats them as equals. She continues to want to be approachable for the people that matter – the readers. It does not always work out as planned as in the launch of *Harry Potter and the Goblet of Fire* at King's Cross station. Quite often it is because she has underestimated the enormous interest that will be sparked by a visit to a bookshop by J. K. Rowling. The literary agent Giles Gordon still remembers an early signing at a bookshop in Stockbridge when the crowd was much bigger than expected. After queuing for an hour Joanne was still a speck on the horizon so everyone was less than pleased when it was announced that J. K. Rowling was leaving because she had to go and pick up her daughter Jessica. Amid much muttering, Giles marched to the front of the queue and demanded that Joanne sign his son's book.

Joanne was more than a little taken aback and uncomplainingly inscribed one more book.

The first year of the new millennium could hardly have been better for Joanne. Besides being Author of the Year, and receiving the honorary doctorate at Exeter she was awarded an OBE for services to children's literature in the Queen's Birthday Honours. Joanne was due to collect the honour from the Queen at Buckingham Palace in December but pulled out 'because Jessica was ill'. At least that was the story. She was actually in the audience at Craiglockhart Primary School watching her daughter's Christmas nativity play. Joanne, who always puts anything involving Jessica first, watched proudly, sitting among all the other delighted parents. The story of Jessica feeling unwell was just a polite excuse, considered good manners on these occasions, although is there a better reason for missing an official engagement than watching your daughter in a school play? The importance of the bond between mother and child illuminates the Harry Potter books just as it has influenced Joanne's own life.

There was no royal rebuke and after Christmas the Prince of Wales invited Joanne to Balmoral. His own children's book *The Old Man of Lochnagar* while not in the Harry Potter class, has sold very respectably and the pair have a mutual friend in Stephen Fry, a regular guest at Highgrove. It was Prince Charles who finally presented Joanne with her OBE but she did manage to meet the Queen when Her Majesty visited the headquarters of Bloomsbury in Soho Square, central London.

The Queen told Joanne, who was wearing sensible specs for the occasion, 'I was a voracious reader as a child. It stood me in good stead because I read quite quickly now and I have a lot to read.' She also mentioned that her granddaughter Princess Eugenie was a fan of Harry Potter. The Queen was happy to have a picture taken with Joanne, both ladies smiling warmly. They were photographed in front of a shelf full to overflowing with Harry Potter books, all with their front cover facing the camera – an unnecessary piece of heavy-handed promotion by the publisher.

Inevitably amid all this acclaim there was going to be a publicity backlash. Even Sir Richard Branson is discovering you cannot be a national hero all the time. When your head is above the parapet of fame then someone with a peashooter is going to take pot shots at it. In the literary world you do not come any bigger than Joanne Rowling who has officially been listed as one of the ten most influential people in publishing by *Book Magazine*. Something was bound to interrupt Joanne's serene progress. It came in the form of a previously little known American author called Nancy Stouffer [N.K. Stouffer] who claimed Harry Potter was derived from her book *The Legend of Rah and the Muggles*, published in 1984.

Stouffer's hero is Larry Potter, who has black wavy hair and wears glasses; his mother's name is

Lilly Potter (Harry's mother is Lily); there is a character called the Keeper of the Gardens (Rowling has the Keeper of the Keys); and of course there are the Muggles, which are little hairless creatures who care for two orphaned boys in Stouffer's stories, and nonwizard folk in the Harry Potter books. Stouffer wrote twelve books between 1984 and 1988 but none feature any magic. She commented, 'I think coincidences happen but I still say if it looks like a duck and acts like a duck . . . it's a duck.'

Robert McCrum, literary editor of the *Observer* remarked, 'It is one of the cast-iron laws of the literary world that no sooner does a writer achieve widespread acclaim than someone, less successful, will cry "Foul". It happened to Shakespeare and it goes on to this day.'

The matter perhaps inevitably fell into the hands of lawyers. Joanne has never sought to hide the influences in her books, and part of the fun of Harry Potter is trying to spot examples of literary homage, to Tolkien or Jane Austen, Elizabeth Goudge or C. S. Lewis. As Robert McCrum believes, 'All good writers, if they are honest, will acknowledge that when they come across a nifty thing in someone else's work, either consciously or unconsciously they will store it away for the day when their inspiration falters.' Joanne has explained that she thought of 'Muggles' after hearing people call each other 'mugs'.

The media, of course, likes nothing better than a

juicy plagiarism claim. The *Sun* declared in a headline: '1984 Nancy writes book about Larry Potter and Muggles; 1997 J. K. Rowling writes about Harry Potter and Muggles'. Joanne is not alone in modern times in facing allegations of literary pilfering. P. D. James, Ian McEwan, Graham Swift and Robert Stone have all been challenged. McCrum says, 'I think it is high time creative writers reclaimed their right to borrow from others, without shame.'

So why have Joanne and her publishers not settled the case? After all, a million dollars is neither here nor there where Harry Potter is concerned. A clue lies in an observation from Nigel Reynolds of the *Daily Telegraph*: 'She has had a tough life and has the integrity of someone who is a purist.' Joanne is very proud of Harry Potter and would not want anything to be allowed to diminish that achievement.

CHAPTER SIXTEEN

Fort Knox

*'She annoys me because she is in some
ways like me.'*

JOANNE'S WEALTH HAS become a subject of great
public fascination. Perhaps it is the enormous
speed with which she has become one of the richest
women in Britain. Every time a list is published it is
her face, usually looking glum, that is chosen as
illustration from amongst the usual suspects of
obscure business tycoons, ageing rock stars and
basketball players. When the *Sunday Times*
published its 'Rich List 2001' she was one of three
people pictured on the contents page, sandwiched
between the boxing champion Lennox Lewis and
film mogul Ridley Scott. A new entry on the list,
Joanne was placed 526th richest person in the
country with a fortune of £65 million ($97.5
million). A year later and the 2002 chart featured
her at number 11 in the list of fastest-earned
fortunes with a mind-boggling estimated net worth
of £226 million ($339 million). It is a staggering
figure, the result of the incredible worldwide
success of the film *Harry Potter and the Philosopher's*

Stone. She had risen to become the 147th richest person in the UK, just 22 places behind the Queen, whom she will assuredly overtake in 2003. Joanne is now the richest person in film and television in Britain, ahead of Madonna, Mick Jagger and Robert Stigwood.

The statistics go on and on. She is the wealthiest woman in Scotland and the thirteenth richest in the UK. It goes without saying that she is by far the wealthiest British writer, with only an 'impoverished' Barbara Taylor Bradford (£85 million; $127.5 million) able to be mentioned in the same breath. Estimating fortunes is a very hit-and-miss affair, but if Joanne had an account at Gringotts, the wizard bank, she would not be able to get inside her vault for the mountain of gold galleons inside. When she failed to attend the British Book Awards in 2001 a joke went round the tables that Joanne was away buying a property – Canada. She *had* bought a new property which, while not Canada, was a highly desirable London residence in Kensington, estimated to have cost £4.5 million ($6.75 million). The Georgian-style house is in a terrace of twenty-five new millionaire homes and boasts an underground swimming pool, under-floor heating and twenty-four-hour security. Madonna rented one for a while which gave the terrace celebrity status. Christopher Little says of Joanne, 'This will be her second home. She will not be moving to London permanently. It means she will no longer have to stay in hotels when she comes to see me or her publishers, which will be much nicer for her.' Like many people who appreciate the value of money because they have worried about it on a daily basis in the past, Joanne is not prone to extravagance and this house is a little more of a splash-out than a new ring or a dress. But even if she never sets foot in the place it will prove a very valuable investment. It would certainly not be resold at a knockdown price.

At least Joanne can still just about walk around the fashionable streets of London unrecognized. That is becoming practically impossible in Edinburgh, especially now that she has had a 'money makeover'. She looks rich. Her hair is now butter-beer blonde – the red hue gone for ever. Like Hermione at the Yule Ball in *Harry Potter and the Goblet of Fire*, her hair is 'no longer bushy, but sleek and shiny'. Her skin is polished and immaculate, her clothes have designer labels and her jewellery is real diamonds. When she walks down Princes Street window-shopping, heads turn regardless of her new celebrity status. If she goes out to a restaurant, then she is recognized, fêted, and her expeditions are likely to end up in the newspaper gossip columns. She is assuredly not Madonna, but living in Hazelbank Terrace was no longer a sensible option.

She finally found the right house a twenty-minute walk away in the prosperous Merchiston area of the city. It is an ivy-covered Georgian mansion that might have been built to protect privacy. A stone wall surrounds it, 8 feet high and 250 feet long, complemented at the entrance by a security panel and an intercom on a pair of splendid black gates with a coronet on top. Inside, huge bay windows look out on a large garden with mature conifers and oaks. It could be the residence of an ambassador.

Yet there is something rather sad about the place. You can imagine little Jessica arriving home from her primary school and having to punch in the top secret code to get into her own home. The trouble with keeping the world out is that your own home can easily turn into a prison. Joanne's friends have been sworn to secrecy not to reveal the address of her new home.

Jessica and her mother are seen only on very rare occasions in Hazelbank Terrace these days although Joanne has not severed all her connections with her former home. She did not put the flat up for sale, instead giving it to a single mother whom she had befriended when they lived in neighbouring streets in Leith. The woman, who has a daughter the same age as Jessica, has been a loyal and discreet friend, qualities which Joanne continues to value most highly. The gift is typical of her quiet generosity.

J. K. Rowling is by no means the only person to have become rich out of Harry Potter. The schoolboy wizard is a money-making machine. His image – wire-framed spectacles, lightning-bolt scar – is a branding as recognizable as Mickey Mouse. Coca-Cola paid $150 million (£100 million) to be

Warner Brothers' sole global marketing partner for the film *Harry Potter and the Sorcerer's Stone*. Brad Ball, President of Domestic Marketing at Warner Bros, enthused, 'It was tremendously important that we create a partnership that would have the ability to globally support the power and magic of Harry Potter.'

Reports suggest that the merchandising and licensing revenue from the Hollywood franchise could generate as much as $1 billion (£667 million). In the UK the then-ailing retail giant Marks & Spencer, itself in urgent need of commercial wizardry, was cock-a-hoop after winning the contract to sell Harry Potter clothes, duvets, pillow cases, wrapping paper, back-to-school stationery, T-shirts, socks, swimming trunks, baseball caps and hair bands. An M&S spokesman declared, 'Everybody knows that Harry Potter is a very good one to get. This is a coup for us.' Toy contracts have been awarded to companies Mattel, Hasbro and Lego, and products will include all manner of things from children's shampoo to Pokémon-style cards, action figures and games. And then there's all the confectionery – including Nimbus Two Thousand lollies and chocolate sickles. A British company, Electronic Arts, has won the exclusive worldwide interactive rights, allowing it to develop computer games based on the books. It is the exclusive programmer for the America Online gaming area which gives it a built-in potential audience of 25 million users.

Bloomsbury has not been forgotten. Joanne's publishers have a two-year deal to sell diaries, calendars, address books and bookmarks bearing the Harry Potter brand. Bloomsbury's success on the back of Harry Potter is the envy of the publishing world, particularly those who turned down the opportunity to sign up J. K. Rowling. Five directors are already millionaires thanks to the sharp rise in value of their company shares. Nigel Newton, the forty-six-year-old Chairman, has presided over this phenomenon. He was born in California, the son of a journalist on the *Financial Times* who turned to wine and went on to run a successful vineyard. He is considered to be an entrepreneur in what is often a lacklustre business, a trait that has not done any harm at all to Harry Potter's progress. He may not look exactly like the boy wizard, but with his black curly hair he could definitely be transformed with a pair of round wire-framed spectacles. He co-founded Bloomsbury in 1986 with former Editor-in-Chief Liz Calder after rising to prominence at publishers Sidgwick & Jackson and through helping Bob Geldof put together the book for Live Aid in record time.

Mr Newton has been careful to point out that not everyone at the firm works on the Harry Potter books and that they have other successful authors, including Michael Ondaatje, Will Self and Joanna Trollope. But although Bloomsbury publishes 250 books annually, Harry Potter accounts for more than 20 per cent of its turnover. *Harry Potter and the Goblet of Fire* retailed in Britain at £14.99 ($22.49) so Bloomsbury, netting an average 35 per cent of the cover price, could receive as much as £5 ($7.50) for every book sold, although overheads would reduce that impressive figure.

Bloomsbury has a deal to publish all seven Harry Potter books and the bandwagon shows no sigh of slowing down; if anything it seems to be picking up speed. In June 2001 Bloomsbury launched a children's publishing division in the USA, which prompted an immediate rise in the firm's share price of 60 pence ($0.90) to 845 pence ($12.70). Mr Newton made nearly £500,000 ($750,000) – on paper, at least – just by making the announcement. Most of the Bloomsbury shares are in the hands of blue chip companies. It is a sobering thought, however, that should the publisher ever come up for sale, then Joanne could comfortably afford to buy it herself.

The individual who has prospered most out of Joanne Rowling is Christopher Little who, at a conservative estimate, has made more than £10 million ($15 million). Mr Little is now one of the richest men in publishing. He does, however, acknowledge his good fortune and has always told all and sundry that the success of Harry Potter was the biggest surprise of his life, adding how close he came to saying no to Joanne because 'children's books never make money'. He has a brand-new suite of offices and a gleaming up-to-date

Mercedes; according to a rival agent, 'He eats, sleeps and drinks J. K. Rowling'.

Mr Little himself admits, 'Harry Potter has changed the lives of everyone associated with it. We thought it would do well but we never imagined we would have a success on this scale. But Joanne is a complete professional and has kept her feet on the ground.'

Those who know both Christopher and Joanne believe they have a sort of father and daughter relationship. It does not get too personal, however, because Joanne has become ruthlessly efficient in her business dealing and Christopher keeps everyone away from her, handling the plethora of daily faxes and e-mails himself. Around the time of the publication of *Harry Potter and the Prisoner of Azkaban* in 1999 he began scaling down his other interests, reducing his client list to no more than half a dozen. These include Janet Gleeson, who wrote *The Arcanum*, a well-reviewed book on porcelain and its invention, John Watson, a writer of naval thrillers, and Irish writer Darren Shan – real name Darren O'Shaughnessy – who produces fun vampire novels for the teenage market.

He has even stopped representing his old friend A. J. Quinnell, and let *Artemis Fowl* by Eoin Collins slip through his fingers. It has now become a huge international bestseller and is to follow Harry Potter on to cinema screens. Another partnership that did not flourish was that between Christopher Little and Patrick Walsh, which ended in 2000 when Walsh left to start up another agency, Conville and Walsh. The split may yet end in a legal dispute over the allocation of profits from the J.K. Rowling empire.

Joanne and Christopher's partnership does continue to prosper, however, although there were strong rumours early in 2001 that all was not well and that she was seeking a new literary agent. Only Joanne and Christopher know.

She and Jessica make another great team, albeit one that was incomplete as they made their amazing journey from a mouse-infested flat in Gardner's Crescent to opulent Merchiston. After her marriage ended, having a new man in her life was a very low priority as she strove to haul herself out of the pit of poverty and depression. Joanne is not a woman who frets about not having a man in her life. She was happy to enjoy the company of her friends and has compared herself to Miss Emma Woodhouse, the eponymous heroine of Jane Austen's *Emma* and someone who meddles in her friend's love lives. 'She annoys me because she is in some ways like me,' Joanne explained on the BBC Radio 4 radio programme *With Great Pleasure*.

Jane Austen is Joanne's favourite writer. She reads the novels continuously in rotation and every so often drops a homage to Austen into one of the Harry Potter books. Mrs Norris, for instance, is the much hated cat belonging to Hogwarts's caretaker Filch, 'a scrawny, dust-coloured creature with bulging lamp-like eyes . . .' Mrs Norris is also

Fanny Price's odious aunt in *Mansfield Park*. A more subtle doff of the cap to Jane Austen is in the surprise Joanne always puts into the climax of each of her books. Often it involves Snape *not* being the villain Harry thought he was and the revelation that a seemingly harmless character is Harry's real enemy. The plot of *Emma* has what Joanne describes as the 'most skilfully managed mystery I've ever read' – the secret engagement of Frank Churchill and Jane Fairfax. The first time she read the book she missed it, as did most of her friends: 'I have never set up a surprise ending in Harry Potter without being aware that I can never come to close to what Austen did in *Emma*.'

The passage Joanne chose as her favourite in the radio programme was the scene after the picnic on Box Hill at which Emma has made a cruel joke at the expense of the spinster Miss Bates. In a powerful scene Mr Knightly admonishes Emma: 'Were she a woman of fortune, I would leave every harmless absurdity to take its chance, I would not quarrel with you for any liberties of manner. Were she your equal in situation – but, Emma, consider how far this is from being the case. She is poor; she has sunk from the comforts she was born to; and, if she lives to old age, must probably sink more. Her situation should secure your compassion. It was badly done, indeed!'

Like a typical Jane Austen heroine, Joanne takes pride in her independence, although she has revealed that she would like more children, admiring as she is of large families. But since being badly hurt in her marriage, she has been naturally wary of forming new relationships. But that understandable caution was forgotten when she was introduced to a young hospital doctor.

CHAPTER SEVENTEEN

A New Chapter

'I think I would have been clinically insane to have expected what has happened.'

INEVITABLY, THE FIRST characteristic of the new man in the life of J. K. Rowling that grabbed the attention of the watching media and public was his similarity to Harry Potter. Dr Neil Murray, six years younger than Joanne, did have a certain Potterish quality to his appearance, accentuated by his round-framed glasses. Nobody, it seems, can wear a pair of circular spectacles without being compared to the boy wizard as portrayed by Daniel Radcliffe. Dr Murray also sported a boyish fringe, although a lightning-bolt scar on his forehead was notably absent.

The couple met at the house of a mutual friend and Joanne was immediately smitten. The drawback was that Neil was married, but Joanne learned he was separated from his wife Fiona, another doctor, whom he had met while they were both studying medicine at Glasgow University; they had married in 1996. After three years they had drifted apart. Fiona worked in Glasgow while

Neil was a senior house officer in anaesthetics at St John's Hospital in Livingston, fifteen miles west of Edinburgh.

Dr Murray is a solid middle-class professional – dare one say, just the sort of chap Joanne's parents would have chosen for her, and certainly more suitable than a boy she met in a bar. He had been expected to follow in the family tradition of both his father and grandfather and work as a vet in the family practice in the town of Huntly in Aberdeenshire. His mother Barbara worked as a primary-school teacher.

He is quiet, studious and hard-working, a solid citizen with whom the more volatile Joanne could discuss her troubles and insecurities. You do not cease to be a worrier just because you have had the good fortune to become a multi-millionaire. In the early days of their relationship, Joanne and Neil were seen holding hands and kissing like any other courting couple. They went out to dinner in restaurants like Skippers Bistro along The Shore in Leith and met friends for lunch at Pizza Express in Stockbridge. She also joined him for the occasional social event at the hospital. Their characters are complementary. He is reserved, while Joanne, with people she knows and trusts, can be the life and soul of a gathering, her Gatling-gun laughter brightening any occasion. Increasingly they spent more time in the opulent comfort of her new million-pound home in Merchiston, where his red sports car was often glimpsed parked in the drive.

Eventually he gave up his mews cottage on the outskirts of the city and moved in permanently.

When the newspapers found out about the romance in early 2001 there was a frenzy of speculation: just who was the man who had captured the heart of the Harry Potter author? An insight into the type of man Neil Murray is came from his ex-wife, Dr Fiona Duncan. Out of the blue he called her to apologize for the intrusive media interest which had, inevitably, sought her out: 'He told me he was really sorry for putting me and my family through this. I told him we were fine. He didn't mention Joanne but I am his ex-wife so I don't think it would have been appropriate. It wasn't any of my business who he was involved with or whether they were famous or not.'

Fiona, now happily settled with a new partner and a young child, added graciously, 'I wished them both the best of luck.'

By the spring of 2001 the newspapers were already raising the question as to whether Joanne planned to marry her 'Harry Potter-lookalike lover'. She appeared to be wearing an engagement ring and was forced to deny stories that they would wed while on a summer holiday in South America. The rumours were fuelled by Neil giving up his £32,000-($48,000)-a-year job, ostensibly to go travelling. His father Ernest was quoted as saying, 'I'm delighted for them and I'm happy for my son.' It was all a little premature. For a start, Neil and Fiona had to finalize their divorce and the papers were not filed until 3 May 2001. If he and Joanne had ever entertained thoughts of an exotic beach wedding then the idea that it might turn into some sort of media event would have had them both diving for cover.

They did travel abroad for a romantic break. Neil joined Joanne and Jessie, as she is called in the family, on the beautiful tropical island of Mauritius for a dream holiday. On 29 July, two days before Joanne's thirty-sixth birthday – which, incidentally, she shares with Harry Potter – photographs of the couple appeared in the national press, courtesy of the long lenses of the paparazzi. Joanne looked radiantly happily, unaware that her contentment and her black bikini were being so closely scrutinized. Even worse, *OK! Magazine* inexplicably decided to include a picture of Jessica in their four-page coverage. She had been cropped out of the pictures that appeared in the tabloid press.

Joanne, when she learned of this, was determined to seek redress for what she deemed to be an inexcusable violation of her daughter's privacy and security. She complained formally to the Press Complaints Commission that the photographs were an invasion of her privacy and a breach of a rule in the newspaper code of practice that bans pictures of children printed just because their parents are famous. The PCC agreed with her on two grounds, namely that the use of long lenses to take pictures of people in private places without their consent was unacceptable. The other ruling related to an agreement that children should not be interviewed or photographed for press articles on subjects that involve their welfare without the consent of a parent.

Tim Toulman, Deputy Director of the PCC, explained that Joanne had never placed her child in the public domain and that there were no pictures of her in circulation. He added, 'The Commission decided that, in line with her policy, she had selected a place that was quiet, off season and not overlooked by any other buildings than the hotel.' Perhaps the most telling observation of the PCC, however, was that Jessica had been embarrassed at school.

Joanne issued a statement: 'I am delighted and relieved that the PCC has ruled in Jessica's favour. I am endeavouring to give her as normal an upbringing as possible and have made every possible effort over the last four years to protect her from press intrusion.

'I hope and believe that the PCC's adjudication in this case will protect Jessica against such incidents in future and hopefully act as a precedent in cases involving other children who, little though they may sometimes wish it, have famous parents.'

At least Joanne has almost certainly ensured Jessica's privacy for the rest of her childhood. The ruling came just a month before what would prove to be the second most important event in Joanne's year – the world première, on 4 November, of the film of *Harry Potter and the Philosopher's Stone*. It provided further evidence that Joanne was now one of the most famous women in the world. Despite the presence of more obviously media-friendly celebrities like Cher (in a silver wig), Patsy Kensit, the Duchess of York and Sir Cliff Richard, it was the picture of the self-effacing J. K. Rowling which made the front pages. For once the paparazzi were legitimately taking photos of Joanne, who wore a sleek black velvet suit and a red poppy in honour of Remembrance Day. She waved and smiled and looked like a star even if inside she was feeling her usual apprehensive self.

This time, as Joanne faced the legion of fans outside the Odeon cinema in Leicester Square, there was one very important difference. Neil Murray was at her side in public for the very first time. For the media, there were so many things going on, so many familiar faces to see that this public outing was not the centre of attention. J. K. Rowling and the first Harry Potter film were on this occasion considered more newsworthy than Joanne Rowling and her first serious boyfriend since the end of her marriage. Neil, also in black with a red poppy, posed in a relaxed manner with his arm round Joanne, then happily blended into the background when she gave some interviews. As to the author of all this sound and fury, she told reporters, 'Before seeing the film I was very nervous but I'm very pleased with it and I think everyone will love it.'

Among the stars of the film, Robbie Coltrane, always larger than life, commanded the most attention. But Harry Potter himself, Daniel Radcliffe, was also pounced on by every microphone and camera. He had already dealt with many interviews, declaring, 'I have thought a lot about being recognized and I think it will be quite cool.' Ironically, he chose not to wear the famous Harry's glasses and was, as a result, barely recognizable.

The world première of *Harry Potter and the Philosopher's Stone* was the culmination of months of hype and promotion which guaranteed that the film would be the most eagerly awaited for many years. As early as March the pre-publicity had kicked into gear with the release of a trailer giving a taster of the magic to follow. One could have been forgiven for thinking that it was *Gone With the Wind* itself, rather than a carefully controlled plug timed at just 1 minute 47 seconds. The lasting impression the trailer did give, however, was that young Daniel Radcliffe was a twin of the original Thomas Taylor illustration for the jacket of the first book.

While the film was being shot, Joanne played a very active role behind the scenes, becoming involved like a proud but nervous parent treading the thin line between interference and concerned help. It was reported that she had enjoyed an unprecedented power of veto over the choice of director, writer and all the actors. She was also a frequent visitor to the set to offer her views on scenes, and would watch the rushes at night.

For six months before the film's release, barely a day went by without some morsel of information appearing on its special website. In September, for instance, the first picture of Harry on a broomstick was released to a public thirsty for information. Incredibly, there were almost as many stories about the sequel, *Harry Potter and the Chamber of Secrets*, with Hugh Grant turning down the chance to play the vain Gilderoy Lockhart, a role eventually grasped by Kenneth Branagh. Warner Bros sprang into action to register trademarks for the second film, including Dobby, Floo Powder, Ginny Weasley and Moaning Myrtle.

Even Prince Charles wanted to hear the latest news, and to know how the film was shaping up. He has become a friend of Joanne and has dined at her sumptuous London home. She herself revealed, 'He asked me about the film. He said he can't wait to see it and wanted to know if it was true to the story in my mind. I said that it was.

'I had a lot of input and although it can never be 100 per cent I think it's going to be great.'

Joanne's peace of mind about her 'baby' was eased by the approach of director Chris Columbus, who admitted it was a 'passion for me to be as faithful as possible'. Columbus had the added incentive of pleasing his twelve-year-old daughter Eleanor, who is a huge Potter fan and would be his fiercest critic if he messed up. Fortunately she was impressed with her father's efforts.

Everyone, it seemed, was suffering from 'Pottermania', as the media dubbed it. Even former Spice Girl Geri Halliwell confessed that the boy wizard was the inspiration for a track on her latest album *Scream If You Wanna to Go Faster*. 'It is a loving, romantic song,' gushed Geri.

Joanne was certainly beginning to feel the intense pressure of public expectation, joking that she would turn up to the première in disguise: 'Look out for the person in the purple turban – that'll be me.' She had become so involved with the film that the fifth book in the Harry Potter series, *Harry Potter and the Order of the Phoenix*, had to be put on the back burner, which was a disappointment to the fans who had expected one new book every year for the seven years of Harry's schooling. It dawned on Neil and Joanne that they needed to find a retreat, somewhere for them to escape the cameras of the paparazzi – the unwanted attentions in Mauritius had only increased Joanne's compulsion for privacy. She needed somewhere calming, a place where she could switch off the outside world and enjoy the company of Neil and Jessica. And somewhere she could write.

She and Neil started to scour the countryside within a couple of hours' drive from Edinburgh. Not far from Perth they came across the perfect house – secluded, historic and large enough to accommodate a bigger family should Joanne decide to have another child. Killiechassie, built in

1864, was owned by an Italian millionaire and Joanne was able to negotiate a private sale with the help of a Perth estate agent. The asking price has remained secret but some estimates have put it as high as £2 million, although half that figure is probably nearer the mark. The estate agent, William Jackson, noted that Killiechassie was a 'most attractive family home. This area of Perthshire is highly sought after with the most attractive countryside.'

Killiechassie is a stone-built house on the banks of the River Tay set back from the road to Aberfeldy, a delightful rural town two miles away. It may not have the lore and legend of the Forest of Dean but it is a popular tourist centre because of the area's breathtaking scenery. Aberfeldy boasts the famous Wade's Bridge, built by the English General Wade in 1733 to cross the Tay at this point (the town itself did not exist when the bridge was built and grew up around it).

The house takes its name from the 'church of Saint Cass' which once stood within its boundaries. The existing mid-Victorian mansion house replaced an older one that stood 100 metres away to the east. Only the lintel of the original building remains and this has been incorporated into a rockery facing the front door. The gardens boast some handsome old trees, including a sycamore where, it is said, Bonnie Prince Charlie hid in 1746 after the failure of the Jacobite Rising. Inside, Killiechassie has six bedrooms, a dressing room, drawing room, morning room, kitchen, library and, of course, a study for Harry Potter. For Joanne, it was a perfect retreat from the madhouse of 'the movies'.

In truth, *Harry Potter and the Philosopher's Stone* was a cinema triumph. Joanne may have been dreading the première but the reaction could scarcely have been better. Baz Bamigboye, writing the first review in the *Daily Mail*, enthused, 'I am happy to report it is truly a wizard show.' At 152 minutes long it certainly packed in as much of the original novel as it possibly could. Bamigboye thought the Quidditch scenes 'fabulous', and added that the deadly game of chess which Harry has to play to reach the Philosopher's Stone had him on the edge of his seat.

Quietly, away from the fanfares and trumpeting, Joanne arranged for two gala charity premières. The first, in Edinburgh on 6 November, raised money for the Maggie's Centres and the MS Society Scotland. The second was held on the following day back in London, where the National Council for One Parent Families was the beneficiary. J. K. Rowling does not miss an opportunity to help her favourite charities.

Harry Potter and the Philosopher's Stone was released nationwide on 16 November. Not every critic was as impressed as Bamigboye, although the film is undeniably a quality product beautifully acted by a cast which, as well as Robbie Coltrane, includes Maggie Smith and Richard Harris.

Perhaps in retrospect it is actually too true to the book, and as a result suffers just a little cinematically. But at the end of the day the film is essentially for children, and there could be no argument with the queues of youngsters gathering to see it across the world. To date *Harry Potter and the Philosopher's Stone* stands second to *Titanic* in the all-time list of box-office takings. In the US alone it took £198 million ($297 million) by the end of the year. After the record-breaking performance of the film, the video and DVD promised to be equally successful.

The publicity brought the original book back to the top of the year's bestsellers. One of the most amazing aspects of Harry Potter's success is how it is sustained. After sales of 135 million copies since 1997, how on earth is there one single person left who has not read a Harry Potter book? But still they pour off the shelves. Every 30 seconds, someone somewhere starts a Harry Potter story.

Ironically, the film's biggest competition came in the form of *The Lord of the Rings: The Fellowship of the Ring*: it seems that there are no films involving magic for years, and then they arrive like rush-hour buses. When all the hyped competition had settled down, the Tolkien epic emerged as the more critically acclaimed, winning the Bafta for Best Film of the year and subsequently garnering an Oscar nomination in that category. At the box office, however, *Harry Potter and the Philosopher's Stone* just shaded it, although both films were resounding commercial successes. With sequels to come, the rivalry can be expected to continue for several years.

As part of the enormous public interest in all things Rowling at this time, Joanne agreed to be the subject of an *Omnibus* profile for BBC Television. The programme was an engaging canter through her life and the most important ingredients. She finally went back to Tutshill Primary School, and delighted the children by turning up out of the blue to talk to them in the easy manner with which she always treats her young fans. She pointed out her room at Church Cottage and remembered dropping her cigarette butts out of the window to try to fool her father that they had been tossed over the garden wall by lads from the village.

Most intriguingly for Harry Potter fans, she confided that the future books would feature more deaths, and that one in particular was going to be horrible. She also admitted writing fifteen versions of the first chapter of *Harry Potter and the Philosopher's Stone*. No wonder it was almost perfect by the time it reached Bryony Evens. She also revealed that the very last chapter for the final novel of the entire series was kept in a yellow folder, having been written on the same kind of Summit notepad that finds its way into a million schoolchildren's satchels every day. It all seemed so ordinary, although this particular folder is now kept in a safety-deposit box and not at any of Joanne's three homes. The days when Jessica's friends would try to find it are long gone, not least because the contents of that particular scruffy yellow folder are worth millions of pounds.

Amusingly, the documentary still erroneously claimed that Joanne was born in Chipping Sodbury. Yet despite the mistake, the good folk of Yate are pressing for some kind of plaque or feature in their town to record it as her place of birth. Peter Charlton, who is leading the campaign, believes J. K. Rowling is the best thing that has ever happened to the place. The local tourist information centre in nearby Chipping Sodbury is still frequented by Harry Potter aficionados from all over the world anxious to visit the birthplace and childhood haunts of J. K. Rowling. They have to be directed down the road to Yate. In the event of a plaque being erected in the town of her birth, it remains to be seen whether Joanne will unveil it.

The single most important event in Joanne Rowling's life in 2001 took place on a blustery Boxing Day in the library of Killiechassie House. This was her wedding to Dr Neil Murray. It was a happy, if low-key, family occasion, unspoiled by the attentions of press or public, but also an occasion on which to banish all the unhappy memories of her first ill-fated venture into marriage nine years earlier. How different it all was from that dusty day in Porto when Joanne wore black and her face betrayed a feeling of hope rather than expectation. Nothing could ever replace her joy at the birth of her daughter Jessica – not even seeing

J. K. ROWLING

MG 015452

MARRIAGE Registered in the district of		District No.	Year	Entry No.
Aberfeldy Dull and Weem		385	2001	39

1. When married 2001 December Twentyninth

2. Where married Killiechassie By Aberfeldy PH15 2JR

3.	Bridegroom	Bride
Forename(s)	Neil Scott	Joanne
Surname(s)	Murray	Rowling
	(Signed) Neil Murray	(Signed) J. K. Rowling

4. Occupation	Doctor of Medicine	Writer

5. Marital status	Divorced	6. Date of birth — Year 1971 Month 6 Day 30	Divorced	Year 1965 Month 7 Day 31

7. Country of birth	Scotland	England

8. Usual residence	████████	████████

9. Father's forename(s) surname(s) and occupation	Ernest Gordon Murray	Peter John Rowling
	Veterinary Surgeon	Chartered Engineer (retired)

10. Mother's forename(s) maiden surname(s) and occupation	Barbara Ann Anderson (m.s.) or Murray	Anne Volant (m.s.) or Rowling
	Primary School Teacher	Laboratory Technician (deceased)

11. Person solemnising with designation	(Signed) J. S. Richardson
	Team Priest St Columba's Episcopal Church, Edinburgh

12. Witnesses with addresses	(Signed) Di Moore
	(Signed) Lorna Murray ████████

13. When registered	Year 2001	Month 12	Day 27	14. (Signed) Angel E Brodie	Registrar

15.	
16.	

Extracted from the Register of Marriages

on 17th April 2002   Angel E Brodie   Registrar

Harry Potter and the Philosopher's Stone in a bookshop for the very first time – but her second wedding came a close second.

The event was conducted with military precision. In Scotland you can lawfully marry anywhere – providing the minister or presiding official agrees – so their own home seemed the perfect answer for the shy couple. Caterers were brought in from Edinburgh to avoid local gossip, and the Reverend Richardson travelled from Saint Columba's Episcopal Church, also in Edinburgh, to officiate at the simple ceremony. The fifteen guests, all close family or friends, were sworn to secrecy, not because an exclusive contract had been signed with a glossy magazine, but because this was an intensely personal and private event in Joanne's life, one that she did not want to share with a million prying eyes. Her love for Neil had been transparently obvious in the now notorious illicit pictures of the couple on holiday in Mauritius. One showed them standing in the sea, with Joanne gently cupping Neil's face in her hands, about to kiss him tenderly. Little wonder, then, that one friend observed, 'They are besotted with each other.'

Joanne wore cream for the ceremony and was accompanied by three bridesmaids: her sister Di, Neil's sister Lorna, who travelled up from her home in Weybridge, Surrey, and Jessica. Lorna and Di signed as witnesses. Almost best of all, Pete Rowling and his second wife, Janet, made the journey from their Chepstow home to share in Joanne's happiness.

Once again there was no honeymoon for the newly married Mrs Neil Murray. Instead she had to resume work on *Harry Potter and the Order of the Phoenix*, eagerly awaited by millions of children throughout the world. The distractions for Joanne as she battled to finish her latest book were enormous. It may well be easier to write in adversity, when a sense of purpose precludes any diversions.

Among other factors, Joanne had a new house to finish furnishing. In the New Year she wandered into an Edinburgh art gallery and bought five paintings by the acclaimed Scottish artist Sandy Fraser. One was of a centaur, a mystical creature from Greek mythology which was half-man and half-horse. Joanne told the gallery assistant that she thought it would be a good omen to have a picture of one in her new home. She popped down a credit card, signed the slip for £20,000, and instructed that the paintings should be delivered to Killiechassie.

Joanne's future, so bleak nine years ago when she returned from Portugal, is now rosy and assured. Her ambition to have more children is likely to be fulfilled soon. Neil, meanwhile, has decided that his future, when not accompanying Joanne around the world, may lie in working as a country GP, and one cannot help feeling that such a life would suit his hard-working and reclusive wife as well as him.

A New Chapter

If one word could sum up Joanne's achievement and act as a spur to others who harbour secret ambitions it is to be found on her new marriage certificate in the space next to the printed word 'Occupation': *Writer*. It is what she always dreamed of becoming, although, as she herself has honestly admitted, 'I think I would have been clinically insane to have expected what has happened. Who could have predicted this?'

Afterthoughts

When I began this book I had a feeling that J. K. Rowling the person was more interesting than Harry Potter her fictional creation. I believe I was right. If you find fighting evil and zooming around on broomsticks more fascinating than real human drama and emotion, then you won't agree with me. I have tried in this book to highlight some of the events and people in Joanne's life that shaped and influenced her as a person and as a writer. Fame and money beyond the comprehension of most people have so overtaken her that it is easy to forget she is first and foremost a supremely gifted writer. The Prince of Wales observed, 'I'm staggered that someone can write so beautifully.'

Writers, probably more than any other creative artists, draw on personal experiences in their work and it has been an entertaining piece of detective work trying to spot references from Joanne's life in the Harry Potter books. I was delighted to find things I recognized when I re-read the books. In

Harry Potter and the Philosopher's Stone, for instance, Hagrid tells Harry that Voldemort has 'killed some o' the best witches an' wizards of the age – the McKinnons, the Bones, the Prewetts . . .' I have in my research discovered that Katrina McKinnon was a fellow student at the University of Exeter and Jill Prewett was a friend in Porto. I have yet to uncover the significance of Bones. Joanne has often said she writes Harry Potter for herself and I can imagine her chuckling over such mentions.

The real Joanne Rowling has, I think, been obscured by the hype of Harry Potter. The 'penniless single mother' story has been told so often that to many it now appears more fiction than fact. I was astonished to discover just how little was actually known about Joanne's life other than the few cliché-ridden facts and erroneous information. It is an established principle that if a mistake appears once in print then it will appear forever. I amusingly found that to be the case from my own experience in writing this book. The *Guardian* noted that I had been to the same school as Joanne, which is not true by about 100 miles. Imagine my amazement to be visiting Portugal and seeing the same piece of mis-information in a Portuguese newspaper. I remember a few years ago an actress pleading with me not to put into the feature I was writing that she went to school with Princess Anne because it was not true. I assured her I would not perpetuate the mistake. The following Sunday I opened the newspaper and, to my acute embarrassment the first sentence of the article included the words '. . . who went to school with Princess Anne'. A sub-editor had written it in without telling me. It is so easy to understand why celebrities can get fed up with the media.

One of the problems Joanne Rowling now faces is trying to maintain a level of privacy as a fully-fledged celebrity. Dame Nellie Melba, the great Australian soprano, once said, 'One of the drawbacks of fame is that one can never escape from it.' Joanne Rowling is now a famous person, a public figure who in a remarkably short time has found her life so turned around that there is a thirst for knowing where she goes on holiday, what she puts in her shopping basket and with whom she shares her cocoa. She, quite understandably, wants to remain as private as possible – especially for her daughter's sake – but fame is also like a fat genie – when he is out of his bottle it's impossible to stuff him back in.

The public has little time for famous people who 'want to be alone' after they have happily acquiesced to all kinds of publicity on their way to the pinnacle. And it makes no difference that Joanne resisted the gimmicky publicity more than most. On the way up you are nervous, grateful for any interest, pleased as punch if someone says they like your film/song/book, happy to don a designer dress for a back-slapping awards ceremony and then seek to slip back into anonymity when you want to buy a pint of milk. Fame does not work like that.

She has coped amazingly well with the pressures of fame and continues to keep her feet on the ground. She is now managing to use her influence in ways especially close to her heart in her support for various charities. In under five years Harry Potter has sold more than 135 million copies around the world. I always have a healthy scepticism about figures and statistics but the extent of the Harry Potter phenomenon cannot be underestimated. As Christopher Little commented, 'To put this into perspective imagine that every man, woman and child in the UK had two Harry Potter books.'

What she has done for children's fiction is another matter. One school of thought suggests Harry Potter has so saturated the market that other books cannot get a look-in. The other school believes Harry Potter has in fact opened up the market for more children's literature, encouraging writers to write and young readers to read.

Lindsey Fraser observes, 'I think any books that appeal so strongly to children are to be applauded and it's been very gratifying to see children's literature attracting so much more serious attention from adults as a result of children's enthusiasm for them. I've been working in this field for nearly twenty years and children's books are so rarely given the attention and consideration they deserve. They are far more than simply tools to help children become good at reading. However, the unprecedented hype surrounding the books, and more often than not, their author, has tended to obscure the fact that there are lots of other outstanding books, writers and illustrators for young people. Jo always does her level best to make that point when she's given the chance.'

Too much praise inevitably produces a backlash. Some of it has been amusing. Raymond Briggs, for instance, who declared, 'It is very galling when a pipsqueak novice, decades younger, bursts into an oldie's profession and has instant colossal success. It's not fair.' Others less amusingly have suggested that J. K. Rowling is recycling old, clichéd, boarding-school fodder. This foolishly overlooks her breathtaking imagination. As Penelope Lively observed, 'The Potter saga has all the prime qualities: a meticulously imagined fantasy world, an unlimited fund of witty and provocative invention, a cracking narrative pace. The mutterings that it is derivative – a hotchpotch of well-worn themes and characters from children's literature – are misplaced. Everything is derivative looked at in one way.'

I would make two light-hearted observations on the Harry Potter saga to date: firstly, it reminds me of *Star Wars*. Voldemort is Darth Vader, Harry is Luke Skywalker, Hermione is Princess Leia, Ron is Han Solo and Dumbledore is Obi Wan Kenobi. Secondly, Quidditch is a boring game, which in no way appeals to a real sports lover. It lacks tension and, if the Golden Snitch is caught after ten seconds, the game is over. I think Quidditch has great visual and cinematic possibilities but I would not go to Wembley to watch it. Furthermore, why do only a handful of pupils play it at Hogwarts? There seems to be no physical exercise of any kind for Ron, Hermione, Neville and co., bar the walk to and from Herbology and Care of Magical Creatures. Surely they should take part in games after lessons at their own lowly level? By my calculation only twenty-eight pupils at Hogwarts actually play Quidditch.

The world knows that there will be seven Harry Potter books which does, in fact, put great pressure on Joanne. It would be enormously deflating if her denouement was not met with universal satisfaction. There are so many imponderables to be answered. I particularly want to see how much more of her own life Joanne brings in. Will someone become ill as Joanne's mother Anne became ill? Will Hermione realize there is more to life than academic achievement? Will Harry develop a crush on someone totally unsuitable? Will Rita Skeeter re-emerge as Harry Potter's biographer? Most of all, however, I want to know what will happen in the battle between Harry and Voldemort, between good and evil. Will Voldemort be crushed and snuffed out forever, will he remain evil or will he find redemption, perhaps seeking forgiveness before he dies, like Darth Vader? One of the most interesting features of the Harry Potter saga is that characters can die. Magic cannot cheat death.

Only Joanne herself knows the answers, and for that matter the pressure now of meeting readers' expectations. And I wonder, what she will write after Harry Potter? She does not have to publish anything again if she doesn't want to. If she never wrote another word, Harry Potter would be a lasting testimonial to an extraordinary talent. Ralph Waldo Emerson wrote, 'Talent alone cannot make a writer. There must be a man behind the book.' Behind J. K. Rowling the writer, there is Joanne Rowling the woman. She may be a little shy and anxious at times but she is a passionate woman of great steel. Perhaps the bad times – her poverty, her depression, her difficult marriage and her mother's illness and death – gave her talent an edge.

In the end with the help of the positive experiences of her life, including her daughter Jessica, her husband Neil, the loyalty of friends, the love of her family and a schoolboy wizard named Harry Potter, she has won through.

Bibliography

Rowling, J. K., *Harry Potter and the Philosopher's Stone*, Bloomsbury, 1997

Rowling, J. K., *Harry Potter and the Chamber of Secrets*, Bloomsbury, 1998

Rowling, J. K., *Harry Potter and the Prisoner of Azkaban*, Bloomsbury, 1999

Rowling, J. K, *Harry Potter and the Goblet of Fire*, Bloomsbury, 2000

Whisp, Kennilworthy, *Quidditch Through the Ages*, Bloomsbury, 2001

Scamander, Newt, *Fantastic Beasts & Where to Find Them*, Bloomsbury, 2001

Attenborough, John, 'Goudge, Elizabeth de Beauchamp', *Dictionary of National Biography*

Austen, Jane, *Emma*, Penguin, 1996

Barr, Ann & York, Peter, *The Official Sloane Ranger Handbook*, Ebury Press, 1982

Clapp, Brian, *The University of Exeter: A History*, University of Exeter, 1982

Dickens, Charles, *A Tale of Two Cities*, Penguin, 2000

Fraser, Lindsey, *Telling Tales: An Interview with J. K. Rowling*, Mammoth, 2000

Goudge, Elizabeth, *The Little White Horse*, Lion, 2000

Leighton, Christine, *Tutshill C of E School 150 Years in Education*, 1999

Leith Academy prospectus 2001

Lewis, C. S., *The Lion, the Witch and the Wardrobe*, Collins, 2001

Mitford, Jessica, *Hons and Rebels*, Quartet, 1979

Potter, Dennis, *The Changing Forest*, Minerva, 1996

Tolkien, J. R. R., *The Lord of the Rings*, HarperCollins, 1991

Who's Who 2001

Wiseman, Dr Peter, 'Honorary Degree Oration', University of Exeter, 14 July 2001

Wyedean School and Sixth Form Centre prospectus 2001

Boshoff, Alison, 'Bringing Harry to Life', *Daily Mail*, 6 January 2001

Bowness, Mark, 'US Author Sues', *Sun*, 16 March 2001

Brocklebank, Jonathan, 'J. K.'s Magic Moments', *Daily Mail*, 18 December 2000

Brown, Annie, 'Joanne Will Earn £80m . . .', *Daily Record*, 6 March 2000

Buckwell, Andrew, 'Potty Over Mrs Potter', *Sunday Mirror*, 25 June 2000

Carrell, Severin, 'Harry Potter and the Horrible Hackette', *Independent*, 5 September 2000

Carter, Simon, 'Wizard Author Honoured', *Exeter Express & Echo*, 14 July 2000

Cleave, Maureen, 'Wizard with Words', *Daily Telegraph*, 3 July 1999

Cochrane, Lynne, 'Harry's Home', *Sunday Times*, 2 July 2000

Cormack, John and Todd, Stephanie, 'For Sale . . . the Harry Potter Café', *Edinburgh Evening News*, 28 April 2001

Cowell, Alan, 'All Aboard the Potter Express', *New York Times*, 10 July 2000

Davies, Hugh, 'Harry Potter Actor Proves a Wizard', *Daily Telegraph*, 24 August 2000

English, Rebecca, 'I Loved and Lost the Woman who Created Harry Potter', *Daily Mail*, 10 July 2000

Ford, Matthew, 'Potter Scenes to be Filmed in City', *Gloucester Citizen*, 7 August 2000

Gibbs, Eddie, 'Tales from a Single Mother', *Sunday Times*, 29 June 1997

Gordon, Giles, 'Egg-citing News', *Edinburgh Evening News*, 6 January 2001

Gray, Paul, 'The Magic of Potter', *Time Magazine*, 25 December 2000

Hamilton, Alan, 'Monarch Meets the Queens of Fiction', *The Times*, 23 March 2001

Hardy, James, 'Brown Slams Old Boy Universities Network', *Daily Mirror*, 26 May 2000

Harrison, David, 'Harry Potter and the Lost Profits of M&S', *Sunday Telegraph*, 24 December 2000

Hattenstone, Simon, 'Harry, Jessie and Me', *Guardian*, 8 July 2000

Henderson, Paul, 'Harry Potter Helped Wreck Our Marriage', *Mail on Sunday*, 14 November 1999

Hill, Amelia, 'Harry Potter and the Small Snubbed Fans', *Observer*, 9 July 2000

Jenkins, Simon, 'It's Yesterday Once More', *The Times*, 13 October 1993

Knowles, Matthew, 'Sad Final Chapter', *Daily Mail*, 19 December 2000

Knowles, Matthew, 'J. K. Rowling, her Handsome Doctor . . .', *Mail on Sunday*, 13 May 2001

Levin, Angela, 'She Scribbled her First Book . . .', *Daily Mail*, 10 October 1998

Lewis, Tamzin and McGill, Craig, 'Magic Hols for J. K.', *Sunday Mirror*, 6 May 2001

Lively, Penelope, 'Harry's in Robust Form', *Independent*, 13 July 2000

Lloyd Davies, Megan, 'Wizard of a Book', *Exeter Express & Echo*, 9 July 1999

McCrum, Robert, 'It is High Time Writers Reclaimed . . .', *Observer*, 25 March 2001

Mulford, Sarah, 'Meet Harry Potter', *Daily Record*, 3 July 2000

Palta, Lisa, 'The Universal Popular Phenomenon Harry Potter', *OK! Magazine*, 23 February 2001

Pook, Sally, 'J. K. Rowling Given Honorary Degree', *Daily Telegraph*, 15 July 2000

Purves, Libby, 'All Aboard for Hogwarts', *Times Education Supplement (TES)*, 8 October 1999

Reynolds, Nigel, 'Harry Potter Rides to Author's Rescue', *Daily Telegraph*, 7 July 1997

Reynolds, Nigel, 'Children's Book of Magic', *Daily Telegraph*, 8 July 1998

Rice, Dennis, 'Lost Love who First Saw Harry Potter', *Express on Sunday*, 14 November 1999

Rice, Dennis, 'Potter Millions Mean Nothing', *Daily Express*, 15 November 1999

Rice, Dennis, 'Harry Potter and the Dark Family Secret', *Sunday Express*, 21 January 2001

Rosser, Nigel, 'Harry's Bloomsbury Set', *Evening Standard*, 30 March 2001

Rowling, J. K., 'J. K. Rowling's Diary', *Sunday Times*, 26 July 1998

Rowling, J. K., 'Did They All Think I was a Scrounger?', *Sun*, 4 October 2000

Rowling, J. K., 'All About My Mother', *Scotland on Sunday*, 22 April, 2001

Seaton, Matt, 'The Magic Touch', *In Style Magazine*, May 2001

Smith, David, 'Rowling Tells Little White Lie', *Daily Express*, 26 December 2000

Sunday Times Rich List 2001

Smith, Emily, 'Harry Potter Drugs Shock', *Sun*, 8 January 2001

Thompson, Tanya, 'First Attempt at Fantasy Becomes £100,000 Reality', *Scotsman* 8 July 1997

Treneman, Ann, 'Harry and Me', *The Times*, 30 June, 2000

Walsh, John, 'Simply Mad About the Girls', *Independent*, 31 January 2001

Weinraub, Bernard, 'New Potter Book Casts Spell', *New York Times*, 3 July 2000

Weir, Margaret, 'Of Magic and Single Motherhood', *Salon on-line magazine*, 31 March 1999

Williams, Alexandra, 'J. K. Rowling Conjures up new £4.5m Pad', *Daily Record*, 13 July 2000

Wilson A. N., 'A Wizard Way with Politics', *Evening Standard*, 8 January 2001

Woods, Judith, 'Coffee in One Hand . . .', *Scotsman*, 20 November 1997

Desert Island Discs, BBC Radio 2, 10 November 2000

With Great Pleasure, BBC Radio 4, 25 May 2000

The Magical World of Harry Potter: The Unauthorized Story of J. K. Rowling, DVD, Eaton Entertainment, 2000

Congregation for the Deferment of Degrees, University of Exeter, Visions Unlimited, 2000

Amazon.com

Ananova.com

Salon.com

Scholastic.com

Variety.com